Advanced Bass
Techniques

Advanced Bass Techniques

Complete Angler's Library ®
North American Fishing Club
Minneapolis, Minnesota

Advanced Bass Techniques

Copyright © 1993, North American Fishing Club

Library of Congress Catalog Card Number 92-85328
ISBN 0-914697-51-X

Printed in U.S.A.

7   8   9

Contents

Presentation

Putting It All Together

Acknowledgments

The North American Fishing Club would like to thank all those who have helped make this book a reality.

Wildlife artist Virgil Beck created the cover art. Artist David Rottinghaus provided all illustrations. Photos, in addition to the author's, were provided by Marty Wencek, Marty Friedman, Tony Bean, Gary Laden, Paul DeMarchi and Darl Black.

And a special thanks goes to the NAFC's publication staff for all their efforts: Publisher Mark LaBarbera, *North American Fisherman* Editor Steve Pennaz, Managing Editor of Books Ron Larsen, Associate Editor of Books Colleen Ferguson and Editorial Assistant of Books Victoria Brouillette. Thanks also to Vice President of Product Marketing Mike Vail, Marketing Manager Cal Franklin and Marketing Project Coordinator Laura Resnik.

About The Author

With a considerable background in fishing, Rich Zaleski has been able to turn his love of the sport into a vocation, that of writing about it. Since entering the outdoor writing arena on a part-time basis in the early 1970s, he has had thousands of articles published. Before making outdoor writing his full-time career, Rich worked in the business equipment and computer industry where he honed the "troubleshooting" skills that he applies to fishing situations.

Prior to retiring from competitive fishing in order to concentrate his efforts more fully on "research fishing," Rich had established a reputation as one of the most successful competitive fishermen in the Northeast. In addition to winning numerous individual tournaments in the region, he was the Northern Bass Anglers Association champion in 1978, and the North American Bass Association champion in 1986.

Rich who lives with his wife, Terry, in Stevenson, Connecticut, has had articles on bass and bass fishing featured in most major publications geared toward freshwater fishing, including *North American Fisherman* magazine. His articles also have been published in numerous regional publications. In addition, he writes a weekly outdoor column for a daily newspaper in Danbury, Connecticut, and is the host and producer of the Northeast regional edition of an outdoor radio program. He has received writing

awards from both the Outdoor Writers Association of America and the New England Outdoor Writers Association.

Rich's work bases on what he has learned in researching bass behavior in reservoirs, natural lakes, rivers and ponds across the continent during the past 25 years. He makes it a point to absorb every possible detail regarding bass and their environments from every available source, including successful weekend anglers as well as the top names in professional fishing and fisheries biologists and limnologists. His primary research tools consist of his own fishing tackle and the database of information garnered through personal experience. He brings a unique, yet practical, approach to his research and his writing by applying scientific-style experimentation to "rod and reel" research. He says, "Fish in laboratory tanks don't often tell the truth, and scientific data isn't worth much from a fisherman's perspective until it's confirmed by the fish he's trying to catch."

Rich has also been involved over his career in the organizational side of the sport, serving as the first president of the Connecticut BASS Federation and the first editor of its newsletter.

Dedication

There are hundreds of individuals who contributed in some way to my fishing education and helped—knowingly or un-knowingly—to mold the fishing philosophy on which this book is based. In large part, this book is dedicated to them. Some though, deserve special attention, for challenging me to continue think-ing and learning, and to consistently question "accepted angling wisdom."

A necessarily incomplete list of those anglers would include the Lindners, Tom Seward, Herb Reed, Steve Conolley and Doug Eriquez. Thanks guys. I would also like to thank longtime fishing partners, Bill Nagy and Tom Zaleski, who so frequently put up with experiments when they could have been catching fish with known techniques.

The largest portion of thanks, though, goes to Terry, my wife. For many years, she has lived with and put up with an admitted eccentric who spends too many hours on the water and in front of the computer, takes up every available cubic inch of storage space with fishing-related odds and ends and tends to occasionally (all right, frequently) get lost in deep thought about a silly, green fish.

Foreword

Maybe someone should warn you before you begin reading *Advanced Bass Techniques*." It is unlike most how-to fishing books; you won't find any "quick fixes" in these pages, nor will you find any mention of a magical lure or bait. Heck, there isn't even a section on tackle or rigging techniques. What you will find is a hardcore treatise on understanding the actions of the major black-bass species—largemouth, smallmouth and spotted—so you are better-equipped to locate them in the various types of waters which they inhabit across the country. Of course, all of this information is presented in a way that NAFC Members, no matter what their skill level, can understand and utilize.

When you think of it, bass fishing really shouldn't be that difficult. What you are attempting to do is convince a creature with no ability to reason to open its big mouth and suck in whatever bait or lure you have attached to the end of your line. Yet, most of the time, it's not an easy thing to do. In fact, there are times when it seems impossible.

Advanced Bass Techniques by nationally known bass expert Rich Zaleski is written for bass anglers who are looking to fine-tune their ability to find and catch bass, no matter what the conditions. To do so consistently, it is vital to understand bass as a living creature, one that must eat, hide and reproduce to survive. That's why we've made the flexibility of bass and their ability to adapt their behavior to various environmental conditions a primary focus of this book.

Of all the popular gamefish, few are so adaptable as the black bass. They thrive in some of the warmest climates in the world, and some of the coldest. You'll find them in warm, fertile shallow ponds and lakes in Florida and other states, in the deepest, almost sterile reservoirs in Southern California and the rock-laden shield lakes of the North. They can also be found in rivers, the gigantic Great Lakes and even brackish-water tidal basins. In adapting to these various environments, bass seem to take on different personalities, even though they are basically the same fish no matter where they are found.

It doesn't matter if your favorite bass fishing involves floating or wading in one of the nation's numerous smallmouth streams or cranking up 150 or more horses on the back of a sleek bass boat heading out on natural lakes or huge reservoirs. This book with help you find and catch more bass.

The book's first section helps you learn more about bass and their environment. Most important, you'll learn about bass as predators and how the predator/prey relationship impacts the location you fish. Acquiring this knowledge will help you take fish more consistently.

Then, in the next section, you'll get into the "meat" of the book: locating bass in their various environments. We'll talk preferred habitats, cover and its importance, and the impact of breaklines as prime bass holding locations. This is the information you need in becoming proficient at locating fish, the most important first step in catching them.

Finally, we'll cover presentation—but not as a blind topic. We'll show you how to determine what your presentation should be by analyzing the conditions faced. Are you on hot or neutral fish? What type of cover are these fish relating to? What is the primary forage in this area? Answers to these and other questions will help you select the bait and presentation that will produce the most fish.

What you won't find are chapters on subtopics as how to fish worms, crankbaits, spinnerbaits, jigs and other specific lures More effectively or how to select the right tackle for the job. These are excellent topics, mind you, ones that are covered in great detail in other Complete Angler's Library titles. And that's precisely why we've chosen not to include them here.

It has been said that in order to catch fish, especially bass, consistently, you have to "think like a fish." What is meant is that the successful angler has to understand how the fish reacts and why so that he can anticipate what the fish will do next. In this volume, Rich Zaleski shares with our members the knowledge and understanding he has acquired during years on the water so that all of you can better understand and anticipate the actions of black bass, and be more successful on the water.

I hope you enjoy *Advanced Bass Techniques* as much as we have putting it together for you.

Steve Pennaz
Executive Director
North American Fishing Club

Understanding
Bass And
Their Environment

1

Adaptability—The Bass Fishing Paradox

Reduced to its basic elements, catching bass, or any fish for that matter, is a simple challenge—little more than a matter of convincing a rather unsophisticated creature to wrap its mouth around the lure or bait that's offered it. Yet millions of avid bass anglers read thousands of magazine articles, view dozens of instructional video tapes, and attend an untold number of seminars and clinics each year in an effort to learn to catch more and bigger bass more often. How can such a simple pursuit demand this kind of attention?

On the surface, it would seem that humans would have virtually every advantage in the contest; our intellect and technology, our cumulative years of experience and our ability to reason should make catching bass a pastime, not a challenge. Why then is that not the case? The answer lies in the very nature of the fish we so fervently pursue. Of all the popular gamefish, none is so adaptable as the bass. It thrives in virtually every type of water imaginable—from the tiniest, most fertile farm ponds of mid-America to the gigantic, near-sterile impoundments of the Southwest; from the cold, deep, glacially formed lakes of the Northeast to the shallow, warm, heavily vegetated lakes of Florida. In water that is flowing, still, murky and clear, and deep and shallow—bass find a way to survive, and usually to thrive. To do so, the bass adapts. In adapting to these widely varied habitats, the bass bends the rules that govern its behavior, causing no end of confusion among those who are blessed—or cursed—with bass fascination.

Young and old alike would be thrilled to pull in a bass like this angler has done. Bass can be one of the most difficult challenges in fishing, yet seem to be one of the easiest.

Adaptability—The Bass Fishing Paradox

The Bass And Its Food Chain

Bass are among nature's most adaptable fish, and they'll feed on a wide range of items within the aquatic food chain. Consequently, it can be a real challenge to find bass at any given period.

Consider the Florida-strain bass introduced into the impoundments of Southern California. The progeny of bass that had never experienced living in really deep water and had never seen a rainbow trout adapted quickly to an environment that is totally different than the one that influenced the fish's evolution. Fish with an ancestry rooted in shallow vegetation and a diet of golden shiners and frogs became predators of the deep—feasting on crayfish and trout. Despite the fact that they had no genetic clues to survival in the habitat they were placed, they found a way to thrive and, indeed, to grow to even greater proportions than in their native habitat.

Contrast this adaptability with other gamefish which have a narrower range of acceptable temperatures, less toleration of variations in water chemistry and a more clearly defined acceptable

Complete Angler's Library

forage base. Place the rainbow trout that survive in those same California reservoirs, for instance, in the shallow confines of the Florida largemouth's native waters, and you'll accomplish nothing—other than perhaps providing a brief fodder windfall for predators.

It is a rare situation in which bass must do any one specific thing. Each time you fish for bass, there are myriad possibilities for success—or failure. The right responses are not clearly defined because the bass' needs are not narrowly defined.

The paradox is that bass, particularly the largemouth, are among the easiest fish to catch by accident or dumb luck, yet difficult to catch consistently. Once again, the culprit is the fish's adaptability. Because of the species' unparalleled flexibility, it sometimes seems any individual bass might be found almost anywhere in a lake and might respond to almost any one technique at any given time. It's why a particular bass-catching pattern is no good beyond the boundaries of the particular environment for which it was developed, and may only be effective for as long as the conditions that precipitated development of the pattern exist.

An incredible variety of habitat options exists within the wide

It's the unpredictability of bass that gets into the blood of serious bass anglers. In order to have a successful fishing trip, you must determine the specific environment that bass are relating to that particular day.

Would you believe you can take bass with surface plugs in 45-degree F water? Bass anglers can't afford to rule out anything when going after unpredictable bass.

ranging environments in which bass live. Given the acknowledged flexibility of the bass, it should surprise no one that each bass fishing trip can be a new and sometimes frustrating learning experience. The mental challenge of deciphering the puzzle for each body of water, for each combination of conditions and habitat options, makes the bass at once a difficult challenge and an interesting quarry. We catch bass one day but not the next, and we have no idea why. Or, the solutions devised for one body of water fail to work on another. Confusion is followed in short order by frustration.

Human nature demands simple solutions. No wonder bass anglers often look for a ready answer hanging neatly on the wall of the local tackle store, or in a squirt bottle, or in yet another piece of electronic gadgetry. Meanwhile, anglers anxiously crowd around television sets on Saturday mornings to watch a "star" fisherman hauling fish after fish over the gunwale. They look to him to provide all the answers in 30 minutes—less commercials. But rarely are there simple solutions to complex problems, and the contradiction complicates the understanding of a seemingly simple pursuit.

During each television show and within each issue of the popular fishing magazines, such as *North American Fisherman*, bass anglers are exposed to new techniques and new ideas. Learning new techniques is fine, as far as it goes. The more different presentation styles NAFC Members master and the more different on-the-water situations they experience, the more tools they have at their disposal for unlocking the bass' secrets. Without a working knowledge of bass behavior and the environments in which bass live, serious anglers have no foundation for catching bass consistently. Techniques that work in specific, select situations are of limited value unless anglers are familiar with the forces and factors that put bass into the right position and mood.

Sadly, a search for quick and easy answers—really a search for simplicity—often leaves anglers with a laundry list of possible solutions and no logical path to connect them. The route out of this paradox lies not in learning yet another special-application technique but in understanding more about the bass, its behavior and its habitats. It begins with the basics.

2

Understanding Bass As Predators

Because the bass is a creature of nature and not of technology or of intellect, its behavior is governed by its instincts to survive, both on individual and species levels. Security, food and procreation are the predominant considerations. Adult bass, being near or at the top of the food chain in most home environments, are not as concerned with security as are smaller species.

So the behavior of bass is most heavily influenced by two factors of overriding importance—food and procreation. Because behavior directly related to the latter factor occurs for only a couple months each year, while the bass' primary activities for the other nine to 10 months revolve around hunting, eating and digesting food, it makes sense to start with, and concentrate on, food.

Let there be no mistake. The black bass is first and foremost a predator. Its behavior is affected by many factors, but its relationship with its prey has the most direct bearing on its hour-to-hour, day-to-day and month-to-month activities. Understanding the bass' behavior or recognizing its reactions to changing conditions is most easily accomplished by understanding this all-important relationship. "Preferred" habitat offers the greatest opportunity for the bass to capture prey with the least amount of effort. "Preferred" prey offers the greatest likelihood of a positive return on effort expended in capturing it. The bass doesn't choose one habitat or prey over another. It merely repeats behavior that has fulfilled its needs in the past while avoiding situations that have been

When catch-and-release fishing, it's important to keep in mind that bass instinctively avoid repeating behavior that results in stress. So, will this bass ever strike a similar lure again? Studies have shown that some will, often repeatedly, while others most likely will not.

Understanding Bass As Predators

stressful or have resulted in unsuccessful feeding attempts.

These "preferences" are entirely dependent upon what is available to any bass within a particular environment. In a very real sense, the world for bass ends at the shoreline. A bass doesn't know things that it hasn't experienced. Its behavior will be tuned to survival within the only environment it knows.

In a body of water in which the most prevalent forage or preyfish is a schooling, free-swimming forage species, like the alewife or threadfin shad, bass usually will be found near structural elements adjacent to the prey's open-water habitat. Bass even will venture considerable distances into open water. Their method of operation will be to feed near the surface. Anglers who fish for bass exclusively in a shad- or alewife-dominated impoundment will develop patterns which are based on finding bass locations where the bass have frequent contact with the open-water prey. It is not surprising, then, that these anglers should think of bass as suspended fish.

Contrast that situation with one where the prevalent forage is crayfish. As the bass resides near their primary food source, they would appear to be holding near the bottom most of the time. The exact type of bottom that had attracted the bass would depend upon the particular species of crayfish. It might be rocks, mud or weeds. Despite the reason that bass came to be near this specific type of bottom, an angler who learned to fish on this lake would most likely think of bass as bottom-feeders.

In typical Northern natural lakes, where the forage base consists of a variety of panfish and baitfish, crayfish, frogs and basically anything else predators can get into their mouths, general feeding opportunities are less well-defined. Here, feeding by ambush becomes more prevalent, and the broken light patterns found in the commonly luxuriant weedbeds offer premium habitat. By providing camouflage, the vegetation makes the bass' task of feeding on the next random meal a much more efficient operation. The angler whose fishing philosophy grew from experience in fishing this type of lake would understandably expect the largemouth bass to live in vegetation.

Each of these anglers is correct, and each is wrong, too. They are correct in the sense that the patterns they've isolated and the techniques they've refined over the years are "tuned" to their fishing environment. Bass behavior is determined by the environ-

Major Difference Among Bass

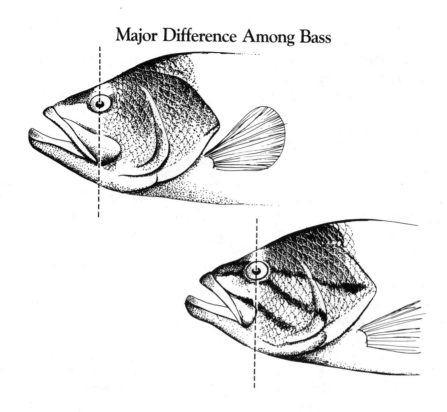

A major difference which separates the largemouth bass from other major black-bass species is the size of its mouth. This diagram shows how the largemouth's jaw extends farther back than the other species, specifically the smallmouth.

ment in which the bass feeds. They are wrong in that bass will behave differently in different environments. When these anglers take their "home lake patterns" on the road, they most likely end up with few, if any, fish.

The three situations just cited are only examples of the many possibilities. In the real world, many prey and habitat options exist. Few bodies of water present a simple, one-option environment. Keep in mind as you try to establish patterns on the water that the bass is far more adaptable than its prey species which, in effect, governs its whereabouts and activities.

As a predator, the bass will adapt to the prey that is available to it. If group feeding methods, like herding shad, are advantageous in a given environment, you can bet that the resident bass will have "learned" how to accomplish the feat. If food in a certain lake is more abundant in shallow water, bass will be found primarily in shallow water. On the other hand, if prey is scarce along the shorelines, bass will find a home in the depths. They are not shallow-water fish, deep-water fish, migratory fish or territorial fish. They are highly adaptable predators, capable of changing to meet biological needs and environmental conditions.

Like most successful predators, the bass is an opportunist, as well. Despite its desire for a lifestyle that revolves around its primary prey or forage base, a bass, unless it is nearly inactive, will take randomly encountered prey when the opportunity presents itself. The key is how well the opportunity presents itself in relation to the fish's general activity state. A reasonably active fish might dart out a few feet from cover to grab a passing baitfish. A fairly inactive bass might not move more than a few inches, unless the passing baitfish appears to be easy prey.

To the angler, this behavior means that fitting together the prey and habitat combination is the key to locating bass. When they're actively feeding, however, the key to catching them is to make it difficult for them to refuse your offering. Put something they can mistake for prey close enough to them and keep it there long enough, without alarming the fish, and you will most likely catch fish. It's simply a matter of capitalizing on the predatory nature of the fish.

As strong as the predatory instinct is in bass, it is not nearly as powerful as the general survival instinct. Being an emotion rather than an instinct, pride is not an element of the bass' composition. Driven by the most basic of all instincts—the need to survive— bass will forage or scavenge if necessary or advantageous. They will also learn, through repeated unsuccessful or stressful feeding attempts, to ignore or avoid certain stimuli that otherwise might be interpreted as a potential meal.

Bass And Stress

Stress is a major factor in molding bass behavior. If anglers want to learn about bass behavior in any given body of water or in certain situations, they must first understand stress. Human stress should not be confused with natural stress. In human terms, stress is commonly associated with worry. Bass don't know what worrying is all about. They don't think about the future or the consequences of their behavior. In the bass world, stress isn't an emotional

Bass will react to stress in several different ways. In this case, the fish's shape is deformed as the result of physical stress. A common reaction is for the fish to become nearly dormant until the stress subsides.

Understanding Bass As Predators 23

problem. There is nothing in the bass' life that is comparable to worrying about the state of the economy, marriage problems, job security or any of the things that humans associate with the word *stress*. Rather, stress for a bass is actual negative influences on the fish brought about by its behavior or by environmental conditions beyond its control and comprehension.

For a bass, getting caught and released or even getting hooked and escaping is a stressful situation. Getting itself stranded in an area in which environmental conditions are marginally close to being unsurvivable is a stressful situation. Some environments naturally place greater degrees of stress on bass. As an example, bass living in a body of marginal-quality water or in water containing limited food resources are subjected to more stress than bass in a better environment from the moment they are born until the moment they die. They don't know it, because they have no cognizance of anything but their own, limited world. However, the stress does take its toll. Bass confined to stressful environments have shorter life spans and often show slower growth than those in more ideal environments.

Exerting energy is stressful, but if the immediate benefits of exerting that energy outweigh the immediate negative impact, the stress is not a factor in how likely a bass is to repeat whatever activity exposed it to that stress. Come to think of it, they are a little like humans—especially teenage humans—in that regard! But for us, it is a conscious (though usually ill-advised) choice or the inexperience and exuberance of youth that leads us to choose instant gratification over long-term benefit. For the bass, however, it's instinct.

Long-term stress and benefit are not within the realm of the bass' understanding. Nature, however, through the process of genetic straining, makes adjustments for instincts that have been exposed to long-term stress or have resulted in long-term negative return on behavior. Non-beneficial instincts diminish both the numbers and the health of bass in which those instincts are dominant. That diminishment is reflected in the gene pool of the overall bass population, and those instincts become, over a period of generations, progressively less dominant in the population as a whole.

Stress, as we need to understand it, is anything short of dying that has a negative effect on the welfare or condition of the bass.

Short-term stress, (i.e., immediate negative impact) experienced repeatedly, can cause an individual bass to adjust its behavior to avoid that stressful situation, just as immediate benefit can increase the likelihood that a bass will repeat that behavior if it's faced with a similar situation under similar circumstances.

When the ramifications of an action are delayed, it is unlikely that they will have any impact on an individual bass' future behavior. The bass is a simple creature, and the ability to associate action and result when the two are not directly connected is probably not within its mental abilities. Nature has a great memory, however. Continuing evolution, or tuning of a species' survival instincts, slowly but surely eliminates behavioral traits that do not promote continued survival of the species.

It is important to understand and appreciate the role of physical stress in bass fishing. A bass that is in an acceptable environmental situation does not leave in search of a better situation somewhere else. It is not so much attracted to better conditions as repelled by stressful ones. Its tendency is to avoid immediate stress rather than seek immediate improvement.

3

The Food Chain

Nature's way dictates that big fish eat little fish, which eat fish that are smaller still, which eat an assortment of invertebrates, including zooplankton, which eat phytoplankton and so on. It's called the food chain. Coupled with an understanding of the bass' environment, identifying the food chain provides important clues in unlocking the mysteries of the seemingly unpredictability of bass.

For our purposes, the bass—at least the adult bass—is at the top of the food chain. It's not that predators capable of impacting the lifestyle of the bass don't exist, but in most bass environments, bass predators (other than man) are few, and utilize adult bass only as an incidental or opportunistic forage.

The location and behavior patterns of the bass are our primary concerns. But, since the bass' chief function in nature is predation, its behavior and location are dependent upon its primary food sources.

Different habitats, offering different conditions, may support markedly different food chains. In lakes with different prey relationships, conditions that we perceive as similar can have disparate effects on bass location and behavior because of a chain of events that starts at the bottom of the food chain. When bass behavior changes with weather, it is usually because of the way the bass' prey is affected by the conditions rather than a direct response from the bass themselves to changes such as water temperature and light conditions. In other words, to affect bass, these

Life is very basic for bass. They will usually go where their food source is located. The angler's problem is determining exactly which food item is the primary interest and where that food is located at that particular moment.

The Food Chain

weather changes do not have to be in the closest link of the bass' food chain. A change at the bottom of the food chain affects everything above it, to one extent or another.

At its most basic level, this concept means bass that feed primarily on frogs, for example, live in shallow water. Meanwhile, in a nearby lake where the primary forage is perch, the bass that feed on them may typically be located in 18 to 25 feet of water. A weather system passes through, leaving bright skies and chilled surface waters in its wake. The bass in that shallow, swampy area undergo a completely different set of environmental changes than the bass that live in deeper water. Therefore, the effects on the fish will be different. Any adjustments the bass make to accommodate the changes in conditions will also be different. Different food sources place the bass in different habitat, and the results of the cold front on those bass are different.

It's important to realize that in most bass waters, multiple prey/habitat options exist, and semi-independent bass population groups develop to take advantage of them. The example just provided needn't be on two different lakes. It could just as easily be in one lake, or even in one bay of a larger lake.

In that situation, an angler who caught bass along the bank on Saturday but couldn't find them when he returned the next morning after the passage of a cold front might catch bass off a hard-bottomed rise in the lake floor 20 feet deep. "Aha!" he says, "these bass moved deeper because of the cold front!"

It's more likely that the shallow bass are still shallow, but not active. The deeper group of fish, less affected by the weather system, remained active. They were there all along; easy fishing in the shallows kept our friend from looking in deeper water.

But, there's more to it than that. The deep bass most likely don't feel much in the way of direct, negative effects from the front. A short-term drop in water temperature has a major impact only in the shallows; for bass in deeper water, it's not a factor. An increase in light penetration accompanying the front passage or a rapid change in barometric pressure, or some other aspect of weather that humans don't recognize, might affect the activity of water fleas or coronomid nymphs that attract the perch and, indirectly, the bass to that hump. If their food becomes less active and less available in response to a short-term situation like this, perch may just hunker close to bottom in a state of semi-dor-

A front can cause bass to change habitats, particularly because the frontal action can trigger action from potential bait. This attracts bass, and increases the challenge for the angler in finding the action.

mancy. Bass that feed on those small perch may find feeding particularly easy in this situation, causing them to become more active.

This aquatic ecosystem is a very complex web. Even more so when you consider that the food chain is dynamic. As different species or types of prey rise and fall in abundance or vulnerability with seasonal changes, the food chain realigns itself.

Certain behavioral tendencies are found among bass in many lakes after the bass finish spawning and the bluegills are on the beds. Assorted panfish and preyfish, from big golden shiners and small yellow perch to small bullheads, key on sunfish spawning areas when the bass and the bluegills go on the beds. Of course, pre-spawn bluegills are right in there with the other nest raiders while bass are on the beds. By the time the bluegill spawn starts,

It's no secret that largemouths like to ambush from cover. The cover, however, can take many different forms. The trick is to never overlook potential cover wherever it is, even though it may seem to be slight.

however, the bass are ready for serious feeding. Those "raiding parties" trying to get a fill of bluegill roe are easy pickings for hungry bass. It amounts to a seasonal shift in the food chain. An assortment of species moves into spawning bays to take advantage of a seasonally available food source. The bass, which have recently finished spawning, are already there. Therefore, panfish are a seasonally available food source.

Similar post-spawn feeding opportunities surround the major mayfly hatches in many waters. Larger mayfly species are a windfall feeding opportunity for bass. However, the fish assortment invading an area to feed on emerging insects is often a more attractive seasonal feeding option for bass. Many mayfly species hatches occur during the post-spawn period of bass. These hatches are also common over the kinds of gravelly flats that smallmouths com-

Good bass anglers know that time spent fishing for other species is not wasted. This is particularly true of panfish. One reason is that it sharpens skills; the other is that bass can be found hanging around.

The Food Chain

If there is a gravelly or rocky bottom, bass anglers will probably find some good smallmouth action. In addition to preferring gravel for spawning, smallmouths also find favorite foods, like mayflies, there.

monly spawn on. When the timing and location conditions are right, the fishing can be fantastic.

Other common seasonal food-chain shifts occur in conjunction with the arrival of fall and winter. Bass species using a particular summer habitat because of its prey might switch to a different prey species entirely when the season changes. It might be the movement of a different prey species into the summer habitat—in which case the bass have little reason to leave—or it might be the bass moving out to take advantage of another seasonally available or susceptible prey source. Or, in some environments, it can be a matter of the bass changing positions in response to non-food oriented needs which can cause a reshuffling of the food chain in the area into which the bass are moving.

The bass that you're trying to catch eats "something." Of necessity, it either lives or spends a great deal of its time near that "something." That "something" eats something, too. Not unlike the bass, its home territory is defined by the territory of the something that it eats. And so on, down the food chain.

While many NAFC bass fishermen consider themselves specialists, they will find that time spent fishing and learning about other species—from stripers, muskies, trout and other gamefish to catfish, perch, crappies and bluegills—is time well invested. It helps the angler develop a better overview of the entire food chain. The more that's understood about the intricate and intertwined relationships among all the lake's residents, the easier it will be to recognize what the bass are doing at any given moment ... and why.

4

Largemouths, Smallmouths And Spotted Bass

Until now bass were discussed in general terms. To paraphrase author Gertrude Stein: "A bass is a bass is a bass is a bass." But a largemouth is not a smallmouth, nor is either one a spotted bass. Many similarities exist among the various species within the genus, but there are important differences as well.

Technically, the species which fall under the general heading of black bass comprise the *Micropterus* genus of family Centrarchidae which includes all the sunfish, crappies and rock bass. However, the *Micropterus* genus is limited to the black bass. It's not likely that knowing their scientific names will ever help you catch one, but the bass fisherman who feels a burning desire to know everything about the species—even down to information not directly related to catching them—is likely to be far more proficient at catching them than the angler who just wants to know on what and where they are biting today.

Of primary concern in this book are the three major black-bass species—the largemouth (*Micropterus salmoides*), smallmouth (*Micropterus dolomieui*) and spotted bass (*Micropterus punctulatus*).

Genetically unique subspecies exist within these three major black-bass species. Scientists have identified genetic differences between the Florida largemouth and northern largemouth, for instance. The well-documented difference in growth potential between northern and Florida bass aside, the two are from the same overall species which means that they freely interbreed in nature,

Black Bass Species

While the three major black-bass species are similar in looks, the largemouth (top) has a much larger mouth than its cousins—the smallmouth (middle) and the spotted bass (bottom). They also differ somewhat in coloration and spot patterns.

and their mixed parentage offspring are not sterile, as are the off-spring of different but related species, including the largemouth/smallmouth or smallmouth/spotted bass crossbreeds.

Three documented subspecies of spotted bass exist: the Kentucky, the Alabama and the less widely distributed Wichita spotted bass. Of these, it's the Alabama spotted bass that grows the largest—by a considerable margin. With smallmouths, there are slight genetic differences between the Tennessee (or Cumberland) strain and the Great Lakes strain, but smallmouths have been so heavily transplanted and moved about by man that these differences have been lost over the years. Similar fate is befalling the Florida versus northern largemouth in California and Texas waters, where most of the biggest fish caught are actually first generation hybrids rather than pure Floridas.

A handful of other species exists within the black-bass category—the Guadalupe, Suwanee and Coosa, for example—but narrow distribution limits their importance. These species are named for the river systems in which their populations are centered. This illustrates their limited range. These fish are not necessarily confined exclusively to those rivers, but their population density is heaviest within their respective drainage systems. Depending on which fisheries biologist you talk to, other species might also include redeye and shoal bass. There is no universal agreement as to whether the latter two are separate species, or whether the Coosa, redeye and shoal bass are all subspecies within one genus.

These less-widely distributed bass may justifiably be referred to as minor species, with the implicit understanding that the term applies only to their impact upon the world of bass fishing in general and not to their qualities as fish worthy of pursuit. Admittedly, as individuals they tend to run smaller in size than any of the "big three." A 3-pound Guadalupe, Suwanee or Coosa/redeye/shoal bass would be considered a giant. Because of their smaller size and their limited ranges, the minor species are most often incidental catches by anglers seeking spots, smallies or largemouths. But to NAFC Members who live in the areas where these fish are common, these less-widespread bass can take on added significance and make up a major portion of the catch. This is especially true if those anglers fish in flowing waters where Coosa, Suwanee and Guadalupe bass thrive and exhibit behavioral tendencies not too unlike the spotted bass.

What The Bass Sees

In this illustration, the bass' binocular vision is detailed. Note how the vision areas of its eyes overlap in front giving it limited depth perception. Also note the extensive vision area above and below the eyes.

Similarities

Evolution has endowed the bass with few specialized characteristics. The general body shape of various black bass, although not identical across the board, is similar. The eyes are set fairly high and well forward on the head, as compared to many species of fish. This gives them a narrow area of binocular vision—aimed at the strike zone—immediately ahead of and just above their mouths. Binocular vision is, of course, a necessity for visual depth perception. As you'll see later, this can be a major consideration in selecting and presenting lures.

All the black-bass species also share similar vibration-detecting abilities through their lateral lines, as well as separate hearing via internal ears. The lateral lines sense vibration in a very low frequency range, and because of their length and their position on opposite sides of the body, they provide directionally and distance-specific information about the source of the vibrations. In fact, the vibration-detecting capabilities of a bass are, to a certain extent, three dimensional, especially when the bass is in the vicinity of objects that reflect the vibrations back to the bass. It has been suggested that bass may purposely position themselves alongside objects that reflect these vibrations as part of this 3-D vibration awareness.

Chemo-reception abilities in all black bass are similar, and, while acute in comparison to humans', are rather poorly developed compared to many other fish species, including some rough fish and most members of the trout and salmon families. Nature would not have preserved these organs throughout evolution if they weren't necessary for survival. But, just how much they use them in relation to feeding is open to debate.

Body profiles of the black bass aren't as streamlined as true open-water predators like salmon and stripers, nor as flat as the smaller, more maneuverable sunfish. Although there are obvious differences in jaw construction among black bass, none of them exhibit the wide mouth and flattened head shape of foraging species like catfish, or the "bugle mouth" of a scavenger like the sucker or carp. Their jaws open in a manner conducive to striking straight ahead. They are, in essence, perfectly evolved for their role as a universal, adaptable, freshwater predator. Truly, the "common man" of gamefish.

Differences Among The Big Three

The largemouth is typically thicker through the body than the smallie or the spot. It also has somewhat less tail and fin surface for its size. This factor may account for the reputation both spotted bass and smallmouth bass have for fighting harder than a similar-sized largemouth. The smallmouth, in particular, is famed for its apparent willingness to put on an aerial battle. While a large-mouth may jump and fall back into the water, the smallmouth is a "tailwalker," often traveling several yards before returning to the water. The spot, on the other hand, rarely jumps. It is famous for the determined way in which it heads toward the bottom when hooked.

More fin and tail surface seems to equate with an ability to pull harder. Of course, fish weren't designed to fight. The larger tails

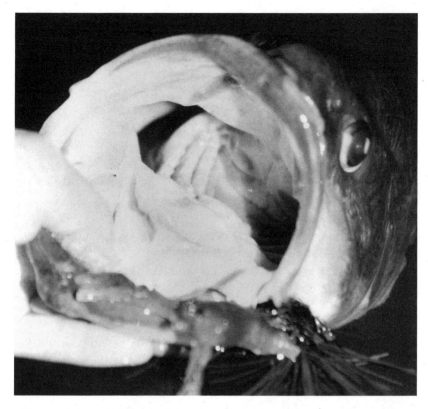

The size and shape of the mouth of a largemouth bass give the fish access to a wider range of potential prey than its black-bass cousins. This is one reason why largemouths are adaptable to a wide range of habitats and waters.

of the smallie and spotted bass propel them at a higher burst speed for capturing prey—a factor of considerable importance to species that do most of their feeding away from the protection of overhead cover. The largemouth, on the other hand, doesn't need that burst mode as much because it generally feeds in and around overhead cover.

The most obvious difference among the various black-bass species actually separates the largemouth from all the rest—the size of its mouth. Appropriately enough, the largemouth has a larger mouth than its relatives in the family Micropterus. When a largemouth bass opens its mouth fully, its entire frontal area is basically mouth. Although identifying the mouth as the primary difference between the largemouth and other black bass may seem to be overstating the obvious, the mouth size greatly affects the largemouth's habits and selection of habitat.

Remember the important role that prey play in determining the whereabouts of black bass. Primarily because of its substantially larger mouth, the largemouth is more efficient and successful at opportunistic and ambush feeding than other bass species. Thus, the largemouth shows a stronger preference for overhead cover. The greater potential forage base that's available to the largemouth because of the size of its mouth makes the largemouth considerably more adaptable to many more habitats than its close relatives. This explains its wider distribution range as well as its typically dominant position in the hierarchy occurring in mixed-species lakes.

Despite apparently being so well-equipped for an ambush-feeding lifestyle, most largemouths still do much of their feeding by prowling the edges of cover, in an active hunt for food. This may be because most largemouths fall into the small- to average-sized range.

Feeding in open water is a numbers game. When bass converge on a school of shad or push a school of perch into a confined area, some of the attacking bass will not get fed. Largemouths tend to group by age class so when they get up in age, their numbers diminish. Three or four older bass don't make a very effective feeding unit, but these older fish are equipped to ambush their food. In general, an older bass is a bigger bass. Bigger bass equals bigger mouth—equals wider potential diet—equals being a better ambush feeder. By adopting a more solitary, ambush-style approach to feeding, these older, larger bass can continue to thrive and get even bigger.

In lightly fished lakes where larger numbers of bass reach lunker size and grow old, these bass could easily continue to feed as a unit along the edges of cover or in more open water. Of course, lakes with light fishing pressure are becoming more and more difficult to find. This is because anglers are having more effect on the genetic straining process. Still, it's possible for an angler with a unique approach to discover an unknown population within a heavily fished lake. Sometimes, fishing "wrong" can have very beneficial side effects.

Unlike largemouths, smallmouths rarely make the shift from group feeders to ambush-style foraging around shallow cover. In general, it appears that as smallies outlive their age-mates, they

Here you could find smallmouths or spotted bass, or both. Some anglers, however, believe that smallmouths frequent flats while spotted bass are more often found suspended off steep bluffs.

group with the following year's class. Generally, if you're catching 3-pound smallmouths, you also may tangle with a real lunker. That doesn't happen with largemouths very often, but smallmouths and spotted bass simply are not as well equipped for ambush-style feeding. Of course, that's not to say that smallies and spots never feed from ambush. They just rarely make a living at it like lunker largemouths often do.

Generally, smallmouths and spotted bass favor cooler water, and do better in a flowing water habitat. However, NAFC Members shouldn't consider this a hard-and-fast rule because largemouths often can be found in flowing water.

In many small to medium-sized, deep, rocky impoundments, the upstream end of the impoundment, where conditions resemble a river more than a lake, will be dominated by largemouth

Coloration in bass will vary markedly, particularly with changes occurring during the spawning season. Here, the female in the foreground is vividly marked while the male is a dull, slate gray.

bass, while smallmouths thrive in the deep, steep-shored areas closer to the dam. Smallmouths and, to a certain extent, spotted bass can thrive in swifter current than largemouths. And in the absence of current, they will make much more regular use of deep water than largemouths. In shallow, fast-flowing rivers, smallmouths will almost invariably be the dominant bass species. Both largemouth and spotted bass will be limited, with largemouths in pockets of slack water isolated from the current and spots along fairly deep, steep-shored areas of the main river.

Accepted angling wisdom also finds more similarities between smallmouths and spotted bass than actually exist. Spotted bass make far more regular use of extreme depths in most environments than do smallmouths, and, in reservoirs, seem particularly prone to suspension along steep, bluff-type banks. In contrast, the

Complete Angler's Library

smallmouth is almost never found far from a flat of some type. Whether it's a gravelly spawning flat in the spring or a deep, stump-strewn flat in summer or fall, smallmouths seem to need a relatively flat bottom nearby.

Because largemouths can thrive in a wide range of conditions, more largemouths can be caught "by accident" while fishing for smallmouths or spotted bass than the other way around. Its bigger mouth means it can catch larger prey, not that it must eat larger food. In "50/50" lakes, where largemouths and either spotted or smallmouth bass coexist in approximately equal numbers, you will most likely find the greatest success by tuning your fishing tactics to the species with the more rigidly defined needs.

5

Preferred Habitat Options

Preferred is a very human term. Preference denotes choice, free will or reasoning power. Bass are endowed with none of these characteristics. "Favored" habitat is worse yet. It not only implies preferences, but actually hints at degrees of preference. Terms such as these have floated freely about the fishing world since men first tried to figure out what fish do and why. It's a human tendency to view everything in human terms. We do what we do—fish for bass, for instance—because we choose to do it, for any number of reasons. Assigning similar thought processes to the bass that we're fishing for is ascribing human characteristics to nonhuman things.

Perhaps a bass habitat discussion should be carried on in terms like suitable or favorable habitat, rather than preferred or favored habitat. Such terms would eliminate the anthropomorphic inferences and more accurately define places where environmental conditions allow bass to survive or thrive. However, the former terms are already in common usage in the bass-fishing community. Anglers should be aware that this particular term doesn't refer to a preference as humans would recognize it.

Combine the acknowledged flexibility of bass with the overriding importance of the relationship between predator and prey, and it becomes apparent that habitat "preferences" are determined farther down the food chain, where they are more related to the needs of the species that set them. Remember that the bass can adapt far more readily to varied conditions than the fish and

Adding to the broad appeal of bass as gamefish, bass use shoreline areas which put them within reach of bank anglers. You don't have to have a boat to fish for bass.

Preferred Habitat Options

Open-water baitfish, like the alewife and shad, can cause bass to set up feeding patterns in areas where they normally wouldn't. Therefore, if an angler records shad on the depthfinder, he should look for bass, too.

assorted other creatures it feeds upon. It is particularly suited to filling any available void in the aquatic community.

Bass filling available voids is an important concept to remember in determining the habitat preferences for bass in any specific aquatic environment. The bass is a universal predator; it can find a way to make use of almost any forage or prey species that is available to it. Where bass are the only major predator, individual groups or populations of bass might very well relate to various different feeding opportunities that exist in the lake. This could range from open-water baitfish, like shad or alewives, to deep-water perch, crayfish and the usual assortment of panfish and baitfish.

However, if another predator more ideally suited to one of the available prey/habitat combinations thrives in the lake, a bass population group relating to that prey and habitat option on a regular basis may never develop. Whether it's stripers or brown trout keying on the open-water bait, or walleye or northern pike dominating the deep perch, those possibilities are reduced for the bass.

In all situations, the largemouth can fall back on opportunistic ambush-from-cover feeding, with no specific prey species to key on. It is more suited to that particular lifestyle than any other predatory fish, and will invariably dominate areas where the habitat is ideal for that style. Smallmouths and spotted bass are not as well suited to that style of feeding. This may be a bigger factor in their less widespread distribution than the usually cited water temperature or water quality considerations.

Shoreline Options: Flats, Coves, Drop-offs

Habitat relating to shallow water and shoreline areas is the first to be colonized by bass in any given environment. They start their lives shallow, and if suitable conditions are available in the shallows, they may never leave. Because bass have an annual need for shallow water in which to spawn, it's the one place in a lake with which they must be familiar. They don't need deep water. They don't need to suspend. They don't need anything except to

Vegetation—whether it's coming off the bank or located in deeper water—is a favorite habitat for bass. It's particularly attractive to largemouths that use it as cover for ambush feeding.

spawn and eat! One of those activities requires shallow water, and if conditions remain conducive for the other, they don't need to leave.

Of course, there are shorelines … and there are shorelines. Bluff banks, steep shorelines, slowly sloping shorelines, undercut shorelines, swampy shorelines, developed shorelines and barren shorelines are some of the specific types of shorelines on bass lakes around the country. Some are attractive to bass, others see seasonally heavy use, and some may never be visited by a bass—unless it's lost.

You may be wondering why bluff banks and steep shorelines are listed separately. A shoreline that descends precipitously but doesn't reach all the way into the channel or basin may be steep, but it's not actually a bluff. The difference is more than semantics. A non-bluff steep shoreline has an area of shallow or mid-depth habitat in front of it. A bluff doesn't—unless it's rising from a very shallow river basin.

True bluff banks often are smooth-faced, sheer rock without much cover for the bass or its prey. The attraction for such bluffs is the close proximity of deep water to the bank. In these situations, the ends, or trailing areas, of the bluff merge with a more slowly sloping or lipped section of the bank. These areas represent breaks along the shoreline, and, as such, are natural holding positions for bass. That's especially true when the adjacent shoreline and the drop-off area are more attractive to fish than the sheer, rock face of the bluff.

A considerable amount of broken rock along a bluff can make it an important area for bass, particularly in early winter. The proximity of deep water to the bank is important in many bass environments when the water is extremely cold. Broken and ledge rock bluffs, as well as those composed of sedimentary layered rocks, are used heavily by spotted bass. The key element is the irregular features of these areas. The numerous cracks, edges, caves and protrusions along an area where the relationship between the shoreline and the depths is unique results in a very favorable habitat option.

By comparison, steep shorelines that don't reach into the river channel or basin—if positioned correctly with respect to available sunlight—can be among the first places where active bass will gather in early spring. The volume of cold water directly in front

48

Offshore structure is not easy to find and, once it's found, to find again. That's why marker buoys play a big role in this type of fishing. They provide a visual reference point.

of a true bluff bank acts like a giant heat sink, draining the sun's energy from the bank quickly in the early spring. However, steep banks without that energy drain can offer pockets of activity along the winter-chilled and seemingly desolate bank.

Very flat shorelines (those with depth changes that can be measured in inches across many yards of bottom) typically are used little by bass. Even with minimal cover present, these areas may become refuge areas for prey, especially young-of-the-year prey-fish. Although bass may not use the shoreline in such areas, they may be drawn to a drop-off adjacent to it, or better yet a deeper trench through such an expansive and very shallow flat because of the proximity of so much food. This makes it a bass magnet of the first order.

In most bass environments, the shallows support vegetation of one type or another. Vegetation provides cover for the bass and for an assortment of creatures farther down the food chain. That means from the bass' direct prey and that prey's forage, right down to microorganisms that feed on the small copepods and insect larvae that the prey may depend upon. Of course, vegetation also produces oxygen and stabilizes the water chemistry. In bodies of water

Finding Bass In Early Spring

Certain bluff-type banks that gradually enter deeper water, as indicated at A and B, and are situated properly to receive maximum early-season sun can be very productive in early spring. C, D and E are secondary choices.

where current is a major factor, vegetation provides a current buffer (as opposed to the current break formed by solid cover, like rocks or stumps). It also acts as a filter, providing an area of less turbidity when wind action or heavy runoff muddies an otherwise clear environment. In short, weeds are good for bass and bass fishing!

In many natural lakes, the littoral zone—the basic food producing area—is made up primarily of the shallow shelf between the shoreline and the first major drop-off into the main basin. Similarly, in impoundments, most biomass lives in the area between the channel's edge and the shoreline. The more vegetated that shoreline lip or flat is, the more suitable habitat it provides for a greater quantity and variety of life forms.

Vegetation forms a more uniform area of cover than brush, stumps and dead trees; therefore, it increases the amount of suitable habitat in a given area. Of course, if the vegetation were truly uniform, there would be no edges or breaks, which would make much of that habitat less desirable to the predatory bass. Luckily, that's rarely the case. A non-vegetated flat usually has plenty of breaks—small depth changes, scattered rocks and bottom composition variations—but a scarcity of prey-holding cover. Those same breaks exist within even the most uniform-looking, weed-choked flat. They're just more difficult to find unless some change in the visible vegetation gives away their location.

Marshy or indistinct shorelines offer their own unique advantages. The adjacent marsh or swamp is a good food-producing area. Its edges provide excellent ambush cover, and during high-water periods of early spring, it may even become part of the lake and used regularly by bass.

Coves, of course, can be part of this shallows/shoreline zone. But coves come in all shapes and styles. Some are large enough and contain enough varied habitat options to support their own distinct, year-round populations of bass, and these should be considered separate, self-contained environments. Others are mere pockets in the bank, more a break than a substantial structural element or habitat option.

Offshore Structure

Offshore structure is basically anything that might hold (feed) bass but doesn't connect directly with the shoreline or the shoreline food shelf. It could be a stand of inundated timber in a reservoir, a hump or ridge in a natural lake or any of a number of other such areas. Bass certainly use offshore structure, but not all such areas hold bass on a regular basis. In general, productive offshore structure have one or more of the three key physical characteristics that provide predatory fish with a feeding opportunity or advantage.

Cover. Whether it's weeds, timber, brush, stumps or rocks, cover is every bit as attractive to bass on offshore structure as it is along the banks. Depending on the depth at which the structure tops out, cover may be a necessity in attracting a population of bass. Depth can be an effective substitute for cover, but cover and depth together are even more attractive to bass.

Obviously, many of the same principles for cover apply when its found on a deep, offshore hump as when it's found along the bank or on an extended shoreline lip. Smallmouths and spotted bass seem to prefer more scattered cover than largemouths. Smallies seem to relate strongly to brittle, low-growing grass, while spots prefer stumps. Both species will use rocks, and largemouths will use the same cover as the other two major bass species. The largemouth's propensity toward overhead cover is lessened considerably in the depths, just as it is under low-light conditions in shallower water. The ambush feeding advantage offered by strong shade diminishes in relation to the amount of direct light the area receives. Even in relatively clear water, the refraction of light as it passes through water reduces the contrast between shaded and non-shaded areas, negating the predatory advantage of overhead cover.

Depth Restriction. Any area of shallower water might set up a prime feeding opportunity for bass in an environment where open-water preyfish are abundant. Humps—places where the bottom of the lake rises toward the surface—fall into this category. They either disrupt the normal migration pattern of the preyfish schools, or by limiting the depth in which the prey can maneuver, simply cut down the potential escape paths. In either case, the predator gains an advantage. Using shallower areas to ambush free-swimming prey certainly isn't as effective as "corralling" them into a cove or up against the base of a drop-off, but it still beats trying to attack them randomly in open water.

Small humps with tops no more than a cast or two long may be worth a perfunctory cast or two every now and then; however, it's the big ones—those that cover several acres or more—that offer the greatest potential. That's especially true in lakes that support a strong population of free-swimming, pelagic preyfish. It could be threadfin shad in Southern reservoirs, smelt in far northern New England and parts of Canada, or landlocked alewives in much of the Northeast.

Attractive Bottom Composition. Attractive bottom composition doesn't necessarily mean any one specific style of bottom, just one that supports a favorable combination of food-chain links. Various species of insect nymphs, for instance, seek different bottom compositions. Most of the very small nymphs that metamorphose into midges spend their larval life in and around muddy, silty bottoms. Larger nymphs, particularly mayflies in the Hexagenia class, burrow into sandy bottoms. Other mayfly nymphs spend much of their time scurrying about on gravel bottoms rather than burrowing. In most environments, bass are not necessarily insect feeders, yet they will not hesitate to take the larger nymphs.

More importantly, the panfish, crayfish and small rough fish that rely on the smaller insect species for primary food sources must relate to the areas in which they live. You can guess who will move in to take advantage of the species that make their livings preying on insect life. Humps or offshore structure with the right bottom consistency to support various aquatic nymphs become feeding grounds for all sorts of fish.

Locating Bass

6

Spring And The Spawn

Bass behavior changes with the seasons because environmental changes occur with the seasons. The metabolism of the bass, as well as the activity level of most other aquatic creatures, changes with the water temperature. The availability and accessibility of food—by way of both its relative abundance and the amount of protective vegetation available to it—varies with the season. The types of food available to bass also change with the season, as population levels of various prey species rise and fall, and as various species of prey grow into and out of the ideal size range for bass food.

Seasons can be measured by their effect on the environment or by their direct effect on the bass. There are three distinct seasons in the bass calendar. The period when its behavior is directly related to procreation, the period when its metabolism is high and intake of nourishment is its primary concern, and the time when its metabolism is low and its need to feed frequently is lessened. It's during this last period that its need for stable environmental conditions is highest.

Pertaining to the seasonal shift within the environment itself, there are four distinct seasons, equating to the four quarters of the year. Winter and summer are periods of slow and steady change, although summer, depending upon the geographic area, may be interrupted with short-term, rapid variations. Spring and fall, on the other hand, are periods of rapid change, as the bass environment shifts from a fairly stable cool- or cold-water situation to a

Soft-bottomed bays with good exposure to sun warm quickly in the early spring. The bass that find these bays will stay to feed, providing a nice source of good-sized fish.

Spring And The Spawn

During the turnover, look for small feeder "cuts" or any place that freshwater enters the lake. These areas will hold active, responsive fish when nothing is happening elsewhere in the lake.

warm-water situation and back again. The autumn change, as the shift occurs within bass from a state of high metabolic rate to low, occurs in conjunction with an extremely stressful situation known as turnover. The spring change coincides with the one time during the year when thoughts other than its next meal cross the mind of a bass. In both spring and fall, anglers must deal with the rapidly changing environment and a second factor, either spawning-related behavior or turnover stress, at the same time.

The arbitrary, 12-month calendar, of course, has no meaning to the bass other than the coinciding lunar cycles that influence the magnetic fields and gravitational forces causing tidal shifts. A case can be made that the cyclic ebbing and peaking of these same forces stimulates and retards activity levels within all life forms. Popular fish and game activity charts are based on this "solunar" (a combination of solar and lunar) theory. The argument that these forces influence—if not control—all animal activity is strong, and there is little reason to doubt that there exists some correlation. Spawning/mating cycles, in particular, seem inexorably linked to the lunar calendar.

Spawn Related

The spawning cycle is the one period during the year that other factors—specifically those related to procreation—bear more heavily on the activities and whereabouts of bass than the simple need to be near food. Still, the whereabouts of species that typically make up a major portion of their diet is of no small concern to the bass. It's not a primary concern at this time, but it continues to be a concern, nonetheless.

This angler has just caught a nice largemouth in a typical largemouth spawning area. Taking fish during the spawn remains a controversial matter. However, this angler released the fish.

Spring And The Spawn

Fishing for bass during their spawning period will continue to be a controversial matter. Whether NAFC Members should do so boils down to a matter of local regulations and personal philosophy. In waters where it is not legal to fish for bass during the spawn, there is no ethical decision to be made. Where it is legal, though, there are some anglers who think that it is detrimental to the bass population, and refuse to participate. They also look with disdain upon those that do.

However, future contributions to the gene pool of a bass removed from the population at any time during the year are negated. Actually, the strength of an individual year-class depends not as much on spawning success as on recruitment rate, defined by fisheries biologists as the number of fish reaching their first birthday. Surprisingly, there is little direct correlation between the two numbers. Recruitment rate depends more on the conditions the bass must endure during their first year than upon the volume of fry produced.

While the public perception persists that catching bass during the spring is detrimental to the bass population, there is little scientific evidence to back it up. However, it is true that most anglers find it much easier to catch bass during the spring. It's the only time when the bass must be in shallow water, often stationary and exposed at the same time. Anglers who don't know where to cast unless they see the fish have an easier time in the spring. Any damage they might do to a bass population is probably magnified by their higher success rate in the spring. But catching and keeping bass at any time during the year removes that particular bass, and eliminates prospects of any future progeny it might have helped produce. Catching and releasing bass, regardless of the season, has far less impact.

The Spawn Cycle Defined ... Sort Of

The spawn cycle might be a little easier to define if all bass spawned at the same time. Scientists who study such things tell us that largemouth bass spawn when the water temperature is between 68 and 75 degrees; smallmouths between 62 and 68 degrees, and spots at 60 to 68 degrees. If these figures were accurate, smallmouth and largemouth bass wouldn't be found spawning in the same areas at the same time. However, this is a fairly common occurrence where the two species coexist in the same bodies of water. Scientific research aside, fishermen who observe the real thing on the water put the spawning temperature ranges for bass across a much broader spectrum. It appears that the old nemesis flexibility is rearing its head once more.

It is vitally important to remember that there is more to the formula than the water temperature in the spawning areas. In any given body of water, some parts warm more quickly than others. During the pre-spawn, female bass appear to control the development rate of their eggs by selectively frequenting areas of different water temperature, if available. Their locations will be affected by prevailing weather conditions. In "early" or unusually warm springs, while some bass seek out sun-drenched shallows where eggs will develop quickly, many seem to avoid these areas, retarding the rate of egg development which holds back the spawn.

As usual, Mother Nature knows what she is doing. If all the bass in a lake moved into the shallows and went into the spawning ritual in unison, a severe cold front could knock out an entire year-class in one stroke. Bass nests or fry "stuck" in this situation are usually in trouble.

In large bodies of water with varied environmental conditions, it is common for the bass to spawn in "waves." Water temperature where they have been is a major contributor to the timing of their movements, but the temperature where they will spawn has no effect on when they'll make the move. If the water warms two weeks ahead of schedule in a shallow spawning bay, the fish that live there are affected. But a bass holding in 30 feet of water a mile away doesn't have a clue as to what's happening in that shallow bay. So it won't move to the bay to spawn two weeks ahead of schedule.

In this situation, fish that inhabit shallow bays on a full-time basis spawn first, followed by different groups of fish from different parts of the lake. The first spawners may have dropped their eggs when the water temperature was in the low 60s—perhaps even the high 50s—and could be in summer behavioral situations by the time the last wave of fish enters the same spawning bay where the water temperature may have risen into the upper 70s.

Conversely, in that same environment during an unseasonably cold spring, the fish that live in the bay would spawn later because their egg development and hormonal triggers are related to their body temperatures; however, the fish that had spent the

Here's an example of a prime spawning area for smallmouths: a flat consisting of a mixture of gravel and rocks. The fish that inhabit the area will be the first to spawn.

early spring in deeper, colder water, would arrive on or close to "schedule." They are no more aware of a late spring in their spawning bay than an early one.

It is easiest to understand the spawning cycle by separating it into three distinct sections—pre-spawn, spawn and post-spawn. Even then, it's difficult to put a finger exactly on the beginning or end of each of the periods.

Who is to say, for instance, when the bass begin readying for the spawn? Does the impending spawning season guide every action from the time the ice goes off or the winter cooling trend gives way to the warming conditions of spring? Or does pre-spawn begin with the first forays by bass into shallow water? One way of looking at it might be that they start working toward next year's spawn as soon as they have left the current year's nests. After all, females are again carrying roe not long after the spawn.

From a bass-catching point of view, it is not particularly important when the bass's hormonal development starts. What the angler needs to know is the point at which forage availability ceases to be the controlling factor in bass location.

Consistent shallow-water fishing begins when more than a stray bass or two starts showing up in the shallows in the spring. But the earliest movements are not necessarily spawn related. The shallows, in general, and those positioned along a lake's northern shore where the water receives maximum exposure from the early season sun positioned low on the southern horizon, in particular, come to life sooner than the main body in most lakes. After spending the winter in the bottom muck of shallow bays with good southern exposure, various organisms and microorganisms are triggered into activity by the increasing warmth.

Roaming fish—minnows and panfish, mostly—encounter these oases of activity and take up residence. The first bass that begin to prowl the lake in search of a meal eventually find their way into these areas, and having found a good food source, have no reason to leave. Over a period of several weeks, more and more bass filter into these areas. It's not so much a mass migration as a random accumulation of bass in the areas with the best feeding opportunities.

But as those waters continue to warm, most of these early arrivals will leave, only to return to the same spot—or one not too different—some time later on a different mission. A strong argument can be made that bass leaving the warm shallows early in the spring is actually the start of pre-spawn behavior. This could be an instinctive move out of the unseasonably warm shallows to avoid advanced egg development that might place the spawn too early when chances of a cold front wiping it out are greater. Another possible explanation is that because this area was found at random, there's a good chance that many of the bass using it in the early "pre-pre-spawn" feeding movement spawn elsewhere in the lake so they may just be heading toward a spawning area that is imprinted in their limited brains. While few researchers suggest that the "homing" instinct is as powerful in bass as it is in salmon, many have observed the same bass bedding near the same spot several years in a row.

Unlike salmon, though, bass will readily spawn in strange wa-

Largemouths will often bed on or partially under submerged logs. In most cases, bass seem to return to the same area to spawn each year.

ters if they are unable to reach their specific destination. In fact, bass taken from beds and transplanted to other bodies of water will quickly acclimate and spawn in their new homes.

Once the impending spawn becomes the overriding influence, however, actual pre-spawn behavior kicks in. As usual, when they are seeking out suitable spawning sites, the fish are limited to what is available in their environment. The relative abundance of prime spawning grounds for any species goes a long way toward determining whether that species will have a major or minor presence in the aquatic community. Especially in large bodies of water with considerable depth available, bass seem to adjust for limited spawning grounds by using them in "waves."

From the angler's standpoint, this means that in most environments, at any given moment in the spring, some bass might still be in the pre-spawn mode while others are on the nests. Still others may have long since finished spawning and may already be working into summertime activity patterns. Also note that bass in the later spawning waves often will use nests built by bass that spawned earlier. Also, they are by no stretch of the imagination monogamous. Females often spawn in several different nests with several different males during the spawning period.

Like everything else in the life of bass, pre-spawn behavior is affected by existing habitat options. The tendency, though, is for the fish to move toward and to stage near future spawning grounds. An apparent sexual segregation occurs during the pre-spawn, as males quickly move to shallow water to search out spawning sites and females hold in "staging areas" nearby. The depth and structural configuration used for staging is a factor of their environment. Fish coming in from the comparatively frigid depths typically stage in shallow areas—often, shallower than the actual spawning sites—evidently to absorb solar energy, raise their body metabolism rates and promote egg development. Females that have been in shallow water earlier might hold deeper during the staging period, retarding egg development until the right moment. Thus, staging areas can include the very back ends of coves, the points on the outside of spawning bays or logs laying in the middle of such bays.

Acceptable spawning conditions for black-bass species overlap to a certain extent, but prime conditions are fairly well-defined.

Of the major species, largemouths are the least likely to spawn in areas exposed to wind and wave action or strong river currents. This usually means that more largemouth spawning takes place farther from the main body of a lake than right along main lake shorelines. In general, they spawn in softer-bottomed areas than smallmouths do. Perhaps, it would be more accurate to say they seem willing to sweep away a thicker layer of silt to get down to a firm substrate. But this may be a "chicken and eggs" deal. Do largemouths seek out a siltier or softer spawning site? Or is it simply that the isolated areas that are sought by the largemouths are more likely to have a thicker layer of silt?

In shallow, swampy bays, largemouths often fan their way down to huge "pineapple"-type, lily-pad roots. They have also been known to spawn on top of stumps, in the forks of submerged tree limbs, in shell beds, and less commonly, on rock ledges.

Don't overlook firm-bottom areas, such as sand (even mixed liberally with gravel), when searching for largemouth bass bedding areas. Even in soft-bottomed areas, they spawn on a firm bottom after sweeping away a layer of silt to uncover the hardpan. If an area meets all other spawning needs, a largemouth may prefer a firm bottom that doesn't require constant fanning for its spawning activities. Areas where the silt is too deep or the bottom is composed entirely of muck are not suitable spawning areas for

It pays to check all the secondary bedding areas for smallmouths. In this case, the angler was able to find fish off a steep, rock-strewn embankment. And he did it from shore.

largemouth bass. The exception would be the lily-pad roots alluded to earlier.

Smallmouths, on the other hand, will spawn in moderate current; only in unusual circumstances do they spawn in the back ends of silty bays where largemouths do. Their best spawning sites rarely suffer the heavy siltation that is often found in largemouth areas. A bottom composed of gravel mixed with fist-sized rocks provides smallmouths with ideal spawning areas.

Secondary smallmouth bedding areas—which may be the primary areas, depending on what is available to them in a specific body of water—include hard-clay banks, shale banks and even nearly sheer granite slabs in a few waters.

In the clear water found in many of the best smallmouth fisheries, smallmouths may bed in water from 18 to 20 feet deep, but the usual depth range is 3 to 10 feet. Largemouths and spotted bass, on the other hand, rarely seem to bed deeper than in 6 to 8 feet of water, and largemouths very often bed in water barely deep enough to cover their backs.

Many anglers believe that bass spawn on relatively flat bottoms. Many bass do, but many don't. While they rarely build nests on a slope steeper than about 45 degrees, beds in small pockets or on narrow lips along banks that are steeper are common. The bottom on these lips won't always be flat, just somewhat less steep than the bank itself. You won't find many beds in these areas though, if you're looking for the classic, light-colored round spot with a lip or ridge around it. The shape of the bed is determined by the substrate contour. On a flat bottom, beds appear round. On a sloping bottom, they are more teardrop-shaped. On an irregular bottom, the bed will appear irregularly shaped because what you're actually looking at is the cleaned area, and the high spots within the bed get swept more thoroughly than the depressions. If bass create a bed on top of something, the visible nest shape is controlled by the shape of whatever object they are spawning upon. As far as a raised lip around the bed, its presence depends not on the bass' nest-building abilities, but on how much silt the bass needs to sweep away. Remember, too, that beds fanned out on a dark substrate may actually appear as dark contrasting spots on the bottom.

Largemouths and smallmouths—all the black-bass species, really—will spawn near some type of cover if it is available. In the case of the smallmouth, that usually means scattered boulders or stumps on a gravel flat. For the largemouths, it could be stumps, weeds, brush or just about any type of cover that might be found in the spawning areas.

Largemouths exhibit a propensity to spawn under overhanging bushes or trees. It's not likely, as has been suggested, that they do this specifically to make it more difficult for anglers to cast a lure into their bed. However, the broken-light patterns afforded by the above-water cover offer a degree of camouflage while still allowing solar energy to reach the bed. Also, in soft-bottomed areas, which are more likely to be used by largemouths than by other bass, the underlying root network of the terrestrial vegetation may provide a firmer surface for the bass to fan down to than adjacent areas without a bush or tree on the bank. This is especially evident with willow and poplar trees: Their roots head for water the same way most tree branches head for sun.

Most bass species will use laydown logs and stumps with washed out root networks for spawning, but there are differences in the way they utilize them. Largemouths will often build a nest partially under a log or elevated stump, while smallmouths usually nest near the log or stump and often hang off the bed in nearby cover when not actually spawning. In areas where there is considerable siltation, spotted bass and, to a lesser extent, the minor bass species will often spawn almost exclusively on top of logs and stumps. Largemouth bass also exhibit this tendency, not only in silty situations but in areas where the bottom is virtually all rock.

Smallmouths often hold several feet and even several yards away from their nests, rather than right over them as largemouths usually would do. This may be due, in part, to the fact that the largemouth often spawns on beds that need constant fanning in order to keep a layer of silt from smothering the eggs. Smallmouth spawning sites usually are not as affected by siltation. Typically, water in prime smallmouth habitat is clearer than that in lakes dominated by largemouths. This allows the fish a better view of the nest from a longer distance.

Although the tendency to stray some distance from the bed is most notable in smallmouths, in environments where panfish and other nest raiders are not abundant, the male of any bass species will often wander from the bed when there is no direct threat. Usually, the male will maintain a direct line of sight to the bed.

Prime bass spawning sites are near some type of solid cover. A stump is better than a brush pile, a boulder better than a grass clump. Building a nest beside a solid object cuts off one direction of access by nest raiders. Building next to a weedbed or brush pile, however, provides panfish, roach and other raiders a more concealed avenue to the nest.

Bass are not "community" nesters like the smaller sunfish, but prime spawning conditions are a finite resource. When that resource is available in limited supply, many bass may spawn in fairly close proximity to each other. As a general rule, though, bass beds almost never overlap each other the way bluegill and pumpkinseed nests often do. It is not unusual in lakes where largemouths and smallmouths are present in fairly equal numbers, for some largemouths to spawn in the same areas where many smallmouths

This angler has found a spotted bass on its spawning bed, near a sharp drop-off into deep water. Spotted bass tend to be solitary spawners so that they can be more difficult to find. This angler also was practicing catch-and-release.

do, but usually not at the same time. Generally, this occurs only in the shallower reaches of a smallmouth spawning area. Any smallmouths that are still on the beds when the largemouths move into the area are usually in somewhat deeper water.

In many waters, spotted bass are more solitary spawners than either largemouths or smallmouths. This is in marked contrast to their summertime tendency of grouping more tightly and in larger numbers than either the largemouth or smallmouth bass. Spotted bass are also more apt to spawn near deep water, often at the edge of a shallow lip, beside a sharp drop-off into very deep water. The right spawning area for spotted bass seems to be a patch of hard pan or ledge near the edge of a flat with a very sharp drop into deep water. If there's a stump or two within a few feet of the drop-off, it's even better.

The spawning behavior of bass in tidal waters is particularly telling. Even anglers who never expect to fish anywhere near tidal water can learn from the unique behavior of bass that have adapted to life in an environment that fluctuates several feet, twice each day. If nothing else, it illustrates the powerful effect of the natural selection process that "tunes" the instincts of a bass population to the conditions unique to that body of water. Bass with adaptable behavior allowing higher spawning success produce greater numbers of progeny, and correspondingly make a substantial contribution to the long-term gene pool. Bass that don't possess these instincts don't spawn successfully, or achieve only very limited spawning success. Over several generations, non-productive instincts become so incidental a factor in the overall gene pool that most of the fish behave in the most suitable manner for the conditions unique to that environment.

In most bodies of water, a 5-foot drop in water level at the height of the spawn would have a detrimental, if not catastrophic, effect on the bass population. In some tidal waters, a fluctuation of that magnitude happens twice a day! Bass typically bed on steeper banks in tidal waters, and in the shallowest beds, the front rim is just under or just above the surface at low tide. The tidal fluctuations vary from day to day, depending on the strength of the lunar influence and offshore winds. A difference of less than a foot in tidal fluctuation can uncover acres of additional bottom in very flat areas, while with steeper grades, the difference is minimal. When the tide drops, the guarding parent moves into several feet of water just off the bed. It seems about one step shy of a miracle that the bass "know" at what depth to build the nest so that it doesn't go dry at low tide; however, in reality, only those bass with the instinct to build in suitable sites have been able to pass on their genes. Successful nests produce offspring; poorly placed beds don't. In other words, instincts not suited to this type of specific environment don't get passed on.

Although few normal occurrences in typical bass environments are as potentially catastrophic as the effects of tidal fluctuation on the spawn, the results illustrate how well the instincts of bass can be adjusted to life in any specific environment.

Both the males and females are stressed during the spawn. The male, which is typically smaller than most females, invests considerable energy building the nest, attracting a female to it and,

This pre-spawn smallmouth seems to be well-fed; however, most of its potbelly is made up of roe. Following internal cues, this female will soon make the move to spawn. Because the angler used catch-and-release, she did.

Spring And The Spawn

71

finally, fending off intruders for a period up to several weeks once spawning is completed. In the case of largemouths, the male's lower jaw and lower tail are often rubbed raw from fanning and maintaining the nest.

The female, on the other hand, has the stress of the actual spawn, often repeating the act several times within a few days. While it appears that the male bass assumes the sole responsibility for protecting the nest, the female usually remains nearby until the eggs hatch, returning to the bed several times during that period. Once the eggs are hatched, though, the male will attempt to run off the female just as he would any other intruder.

Accepted angling wisdom is that neither the male nor the female will eat during the spawning period. Accepted angling wisdom is only partially right. Males do not show any hesitancy to feed during the period when they are cruising the shallows in search of spawning sites and building nests. At the same time, staging females also feed actively and aggressively. Once they become involved in trying to attract a female into the nest, however, males become single-minded, showing little interest in feeding. Females, on the other hand, continue to eat, but primarily on an opportunistic basis rather than actually hunting for food.

During the time that bass are actually spawning—when both the male and female bass are present on the bed—they are virtually unaware of their surroundings. They can't be tempted readily to take a meal or to react to any external stimuli, for that matter.

Once the actual spawning process is complete, the male becomes extremely protective of the nest site, and will attack almost anything that it considers threatening. Many males will eat some of the smaller nest raiders rather than simply driving them from the nest. During this same period, the female may lie low for a day or two before becoming involved with another male or turning her attentions to prey.

Fishing extremely heavy overhead cover near the nests for active males can often produce a giant female or two, as well. A dock, a fallen tree or, better yet, a tangle of submerged logs is the ideal place to flip a large, slow-moving lure like a jig and pork frog or plastic lizard. The "recuperating" female will take a shot at a potential meal if she can take it with minimal exertion.

The post-spawn period, regarded in some sections of the country as one of the toughest times of the year to catch bass, begins

Complete Angler's Library

A combination of the best available feeding opportunity for the bass and a seasonal abundance of prey makes the post-spawn period opportune for anglers to use soft stickbaits which are good imitations of injured prey.

Spring And The Spawn

Fishing for bass during the post-spawn period can produce nice fish, as indicated here, but it can test an angler's capability as an angler. One reason is the abundance of food that usually accompanies this period.

when fish are done with their spawning and nest-protecting activities. In reality, both males and females of all the bass species feed very heavily during the post-spawn. But in many environments, this is also the time of the year when food is most abundant, making it considerably more difficult to get a bass to take your bait.

Post-spawn behavior is often centered around what is currently the best feeding opportunity, and when that opportunity ends, the fish disperse and work into their established summer behavior patterns. That "best seasonal feeding opportunity" is, like everything else in the life of a bass, specific to certain bodies of water and dependent upon seasonal conditions.

In many waters, bass that have recently moved off the nests move a short distance to where sunfish—recent raiders of the bass nests—are now spawning. They're not necessarily keying on the sunfish, but on the small bullheads, perch, crayfish and other aquatic creatures that invariably gather to make life miserable for the spawning sunnies. Female bass, in particular, seem to exhibit this particular form of post-spawn behavior—often while males are still guarding their nests. This behavior is, of course, most prevalent in lakes in which sunfish or bluegill, as well as other assorted nest raiders, are abundant and aggressive.

Other common post-spawn behavior patterns related to feeding include taking advantage of mayfly hatches that so often coincide with this period, and "stacking up" on the first major depth break outside spawning bays to key on free swimming prey. In the first instance, mid-depth (8 to 20 feet) sand/mud flats adjacent to the spawning areas are the key. In the second, you're looking for a near-vertical drop, such as a tight outside bend in a main lake creek channel that swings close to the mouth of the spawning bay.

In all cases, post-spawn activity is keyed to an extraordinary abundance of some type of prey which is reasonably close to the spawning grounds. It doesn't have to be and, in fact, often isn't the same prey species that the bass feed upon during the rest of the year. If a seasonal windfall feeding opportunity occurs when spawning is winding down, you can bet that the bass in the area will take advantage of it.

7

Summer Through Winter

Summer is a time of comparative stability for bass. The water is warm and gets warmer by the day. As long as weather patterns remain seasonally appropriate, activity remains fairly constant, and most bass do little in the way of long-range movements or shifting behavior patterns. The most successful bass in any environment will "own" the areas with the best food production in terms of abundance and vulnerability. They live in areas that fulfill all their needs. Once they establish behavior patterns that allow them to capitalize on the feeding opportunities offered in those areas, they have little need to make wholesale changes. When conditions do take a turn for the worse, they simply lower their activity level in order to survive.

There was a time, not all that long ago, really, when midsummer was considered the dog days, a tough time to catch fish. Myths and the fisherman's tall tales explaining why fishing was difficult in the summer abounded. In various locales, angling lore held that bass hibernated during the summer, lost their appetites in warm water, or their teeth fell out.

Science has since taken those excuses away from us by teaching us that bass, like other cold-blooded creatures, actually eat more during the warmest months. Their need for nourishment is directly related to their body's metabolism, and warmer water means a higher body temperature along with a correspondingly higher metabolic rate. They digest food faster, use up energy faster; therefore, they must eat more often. Also during the sum-

Here's a bass taken during the notorious fall-feeding blitz. Does it mean that the bass are instinctively fattening up for winter? Or is it just a case of the bass trying to get through the turnover? Anglers must answer these questions.

Summer Through Winter

mer, prey is more abundant, which simply reduces the odds that a bass or any other fish's next meal will be one with a hook in it. Fortunately, the odds can be tilted back in the angler's favor by fishing intelligently.

Intelligent fishing includes analyzing the available bass habitat, making educated judgments as to how potential prey fit into that habitat, applying your knowledge of bass behavior and feeding patterns to that information, and using all this information to determine the right spot to fish. Each trip—whether it's a successful or unsuccessful fishing experience—plays a part in helping anglers refine their abilities to define the factors that influence bass location and activity. Finally, and perhaps most important of all, intelligent fishing includes remaining flexible in making these judgments.

Fishing is a lot like troubleshooting. Look at the conditions, come up with a most likely scenario based on your interpretation of all the cumulative knowledge at your disposal, and act accordingly. The success or lack of success from your initial efforts guides the adjustments you continue to make until the problem is solved. Every strategy conceived—every cast made, actually—should be more than an attempt to catch a fish. It should also act as a probe, helping uncover additional information for defining new strategies and refining techniques for those particular conditions.

The advantages of fishing intelligently apply to all seasons, but are particularly important in the summer. This is when nature imposes fewer limits on what bass might or might not do. In spring, as outlined in the previous chapter, NAFC Members can reasonably expect to find bass most days either in, headed toward or holding near their spawning areas. In the fall, their activity is influenced by the effects of turnover, while in winter, their lower metabolism helps define and limit the most likely techniques and areas. But in summer, more different types of food are available, and more activity and suitable habitat options exist. Thus, there are more potential solutions to the bass-fishing challenge which means more combinations of location and presentation to sift through in order to come up with the best answer for any given day on any given body of water.

The bass' need to feed frequently in warm water mandates that it spend as much of its time as possible where there is as much food as possible. Flats, whether along the shoreline shelf or on an off-

Bass Locations In Summer

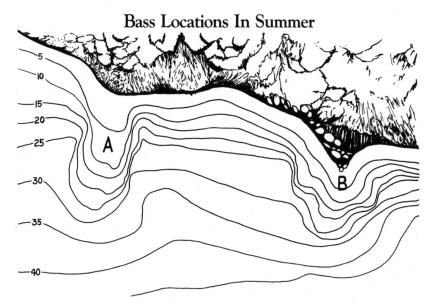

Point A with its more expansive food-shelf area probably will be more productive during summer than point B, despite B's sharper drop into deep water. However, these factors make B a better cold-water choice.

shore hump, represent the most fertile food producing areas in a lake. There are exceptions, of course, but in many environments, flats best fit the bass' summertime needs.

Just because summer bass relate to flats doesn't necessarily mean you're likely to find them in the middle of any large expanse of flat bottom. The propensity for bass to use and relate to structure remains constant. The edges, breaks and breaklines associated with the flats are the places to concentrate your efforts, but the size and quality of the food shelf becomes a major factor in how potentially productive a structure is. Two adjacent and basically similar points should be judged on the food-producing potential of their horizontal components. This is before considering the severity of the drop-off at the edge of the flat or the flat's proximity to the deepest water in the lake, or how well it fits into your favorite fishing techniques.

Of course, cover enters into this mix as well. Vegetated flats or those with a lot of stumps or brush can hold more food than similar, sparsely covered flats, as well as providing more ambush feeding positions. The more types of cover on a flat, the better. One expansive bed of milfoil isn't as attractive a habitat option to bass as a milfoil bed with a mixture of patches of eelgrass or cabbage, a few scattered boulders or a line of stumps.

How the flat is situated in relation to probable paths of baitfish movements must also be taken into account. In lakes where shad or alewife are important prey, much of the early-morning and late-evening activity will be centered around the outside edges of the weedbeds or cover-strewn flats. That's where those open-water baitfish make contact as they move toward and into the shallows during the low-light periods. Midday bass fishing in these same waters is often a matter of fishing deeper in the heaviest cover on the flats or checking offshore humps—especially those that are large enough and shallow enough to disrupt the normal movements of those baitfish schools in open water.

Of course, where crayfish are a factor, which includes the vast majority of bass-holding waters in the country, they will play a role in the habitat preferences of at least some of the bass, some of the time. Depending on where you happen to be in the country and, correspondingly, what the predominant type of crayfish is, this could mean expending extra effort on riprap banks, gravel shoals, mud or clay banks or even weedbeds.

The Fall Cooling Period

In a bass lake, the stable conditions of the warm water of summer don't just give way to winter in a gradual flow. The change may or may not be abrupt, but it is almost invariably tumultuous. Understanding the process that is called turnover is a simple matter of physics. Understanding its effects on the bass and their environment is far more complex. It's best to tackle the straightforward part first.

Most materials contract as the material's temperature drops. Water, though, has the unique property of being most dense at approximately 39 degrees F. As water cools toward this temperature, it becomes more dense (heavier). As it cools below that point, it starts to expand again. No one is more thankful for this property than the antifreeze industry—except perhaps aquatic creatures. The existence of these creatures would be impossible were it not for this factor. (Water would freeze uniformly, instead of from the surface down.)

Both heating and cooling of the water takes place from the surface. In the summer, the surface water becomes lighter. The

Fall Turnover Simplified

← (Prevailing Wind)

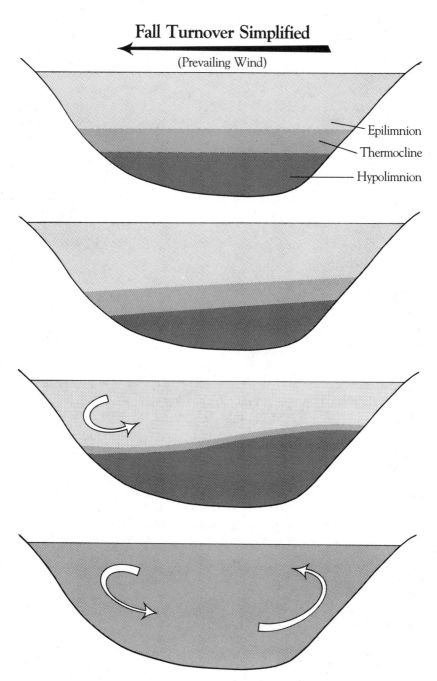

Epilimnion
Thermocline
Hypolimnion

This shows in detail the steps that occur when a lake's late-season turnover takes place. The process starts in late summer in most areas and continues through early winter. In the second and third phases, the wind "piles" the warm-water layer at one side, forcing the fall turnover.

warmest water remains at the top, and continues to get warmer as it's exposed to summer's long, daily periods of sunlight. Water circulation in non-flowing and slow-flowing environments is produced primarily by wind action which has the most effect on surface and near-surface waters. Except in very shallow areas, the bottom of the lake receives little if any of the solar energy. Below the depth at which surface-oriented currents mix the water, heat transfer takes place only by conduction.

The layer of cold water on the lake bottom and the warm-water layer at the surface are separated by a band of water called the thermocline. The thermocline serves to prevent circulation of the bottom layer of water with the top. For all practical purposes, the water beneath the thermocline which forms in early summer remains trapped there.

To paraphrase an old military saying into more genteel terms, "Organic waste flows downhill." Oxygen-consuming waste products filter down to the bottom of the lake, and much of it reaches into the deep basin (beneath the thermocline) where it accumulates as silt. Depending upon the overall fertility of the lake (and, correspondingly, the amount of organic waste produced), the trapped water beneath the thermocline may become virtually devoid of dissolved oxygen by late summer. Additionally, the decay of the basin silt's organic component actually creates poisonous methane, and much of that remains trapped in the stagnant layer beneath the thermocline as well. In a moderately to very fertile lake, this deep layer of water, the hypolimnion, can often be a decidedly unhealthy place.

The end of summer and the accompanying shorter daylight periods, combined with the frequent passage of cold fronts, take their toll on surface-water temperature. As thermal energy is lost into the atmosphere, the surface temperature drops. Of course, this causes the surface water to become more dense, and the surface layer sinks through the slightly less dense water beneath it. Circulation of water based on its temperature-related density is called convection. Keep in mind that just because convection is occurring doesn't mean that conduction ceases. As that now-cooler water starts to sink, it absorbs heat from the water immediately beneath it. The result is a gradual cooling of the epilimnion or upper layer of water.

This is the period—the fall cooling trend preceding turn-

Laboratory tests indicate that most bass become virtually dormant in water colder than 40 to 45 degrees. The paradox is that it contradicts the exceptional cold-water fishing in the northern part of the bass' range.

over—that brings the infamous fall-feeding blitz among bass. Angling lore has it that the fish are fattening themselves up for winter. Such advance preparation is most likely outside the limited mental capacities of bass because they don't "know" about winter. However, bass that feed heavily during the early part of the cooling trend obviously have a better chance of surviving what's to come. Survival of bass with this instinct molds future generations. Bass that don't survive this situation obviously can't pass on their genes to new generations. Bass that just barely survive may still have the ability to pass on their genes, but they may not be healthy or strong enough to ensure high nesting and fry protection success. Behavioral instincts that don't lend themselves to these conditions are weeded out of the population over a period of generations through this natural, selective breeding filter which effectively emphasizes the surviving instincts.

Although nature has not provided bass with the ability to reason, it does use repetition as a device to give acquired behavioral tendencies the same kind of force as inbred instincts. Perhaps that's why it often seems that the largest (usually the oldest) bass are the most active during the first cooling period of the late summer and early fall. This only comes once a year so perhaps only older bass will have experienced it enough to have "learned" from it. In any case, if the bass are getting ready for anything, it's most likely the turnover—not the winter.

As already indicated, the upper layer of water cools slowly and evenly. Eventually, all the water above the thermocline is the same temperature as the water at the top of the thermocline. Continued cooling starts breaking down the 'cline. Remember that a lot of garbage is trapped beneath the 'cline, including oxygen-depleted and possibly methane-contaminated water.

When the thermocline thins and the pressure from a strong wind piles water on one side of the lake causing the 'cline to rupture, the actual turnover begins. With the convection-inhibiting thermocline gone, all that unhealthy water is free to mix with the oxygenated water from above. In short order, the lake temporarily becomes a considerably less hospitable environment for bass and for virtually every other living thing in the lake.

Being adaptable creatures, bass exhibit a variety of different reactions to the sudden arrival of tough—even life threatening—conditions. These reactions depend largely on where the bass are located within the lake. Bass in the upriver end of impoundments aren't affected at all! The normal current keeps the water in a constant state of circulation, preventing stratification. Without stratification, there can be no turnover, so all that these bass experience is dropping water temperatures. Bass that resided near the river-like section of the lake may actually move into the more stable conditions afforded by the flowing water at this time.

Bass living in the shallows along the windward shore are less likely to experience any major hardship because the already oxygenated surface waters are being blown toward the shore area by the prevailing winds. If anything, they'll move tighter to the bank where the oxygen content is likely to be higher.

Likewise, bass in the back ends of coves or any place freshwater enters the lake will move farther into the freshwater flow, es-

During the fall turnover, many bass will remain unaffected by it—particularly those that are in the shallows. So find those spots and fish them hard. Bad weather helps because it speeds up the turnover process and brings a quicker end to the turnover fishing blues.

caping the main lake's less-than-desirable conditions.

Productive fishing strategies can be built around capitalizing on these various "turnover avoidance" behavior patterns; however, the bulk of a lake's bass population is rarely involved. Most bass are left to fend for themselves. The typical reaction of these bass is to kick their metabolisms into low gear, find a reasonably secure position and remain there in a near-dormant state. This activity mode—a non-activity mode really—will be discussed later when activity levels in general are covered. The point to be made here is that during the turnover's height, fish those spots or areas where the turnover has little effect.

In easing the pain of the turnover, bad weather can be a blessing. The colder, windier and all-round nastier the weather is in the days immediately following turnover, the faster the water will be refreshed and cleansed by wave action and convection-driven circulation, and the sooner the difficult fishing will end. This is one time of the year when bass fishermen don't want to see (or shouldn't want to see) a warm front. Pleasant weather conditions will only postpone the return of stable water conditions and predictable bass activity.

The Cold-Water Season

In the extreme southern end of bassdom in the U.S., the "cold-water" cycle may last only a few weeks—if it occurs at all. At the northern extreme, it might occupy six months. Bass adapt. Anglers must, too.

Once the turnover is completed and the lake water is rejuvenated, the cold-water season sets in. This typically coincides with water temperatures dropping into the 40s. However, there's no designated water temperature that can be applied to this occurrence because the turnover is tied to the water temperature at the thermocline's base. This can vary widely according to latitude and even from lake to lake within a contiguous geographical area.

Several laboratory studies show a tendency among bass to refuse food when the water temperature (and their body temperature) drops into the 40s. However, these studies' results may be the product of a disparity between laboratory testing and the real world's "rod and reel research" rather than identification of a biological trait attributable to the bass.

In latitudes where water temperatures normally drop into the 30s for long periods each year, the time between turnover recovery and ice-up is among the most consistent bass-fishing periods of the year! Yet in the southern half of the nation, fishing for bass—particularly largemouth bass—is considered extra-tough when the water temperature dips into even the mid-40s. Is this an example of evolution or adaptation to specific environments? Or could it be just a matter of the detrimental effects of turnover starting later and lasting longer in the milder Southern climate, with no extended period of stable conditions and increased bass activity following it?

As stated previously, in cold water, the metabolic rate of a bass is slow. The bass digests food slowly and feeds infrequently. Perhaps in latitudes where exceptional cold-water bass catches are commonplace, it is more a matter of mass exposure than strong

Because bass can be caught in cold waters, anglers question whether these fish really become dormant. In theory, bass under the ice should be incapable of taking bait; however, if the angler is patient and has the right presentation, they will take it.

fish activity. In late fall, so many bass get tightly grouped into small areas in some Northern waters that any slow-moving, bottom-hugging lure gets dragged past enough fish during the course of a day to overcome possibly listless feeding attitudes.

The lower the metabolism rate is, the longer it takes a bass to adjust to changes in its environment. Long periods of being "out of sync" with existing conditions represent a form of physical stress. As already established, bass movements are more related to avoiding physically stressful situations than being attracted to conditions that might be closer to ideal. Bass in a harsh environment will opt for stability over conditions that are slightly closer to ideal but subject to frequent fluctuations in temperature or chemistry. If the environment in any specific body of water becomes extremely harsh, a high percentage of its bass population will search out areas to insulate them from fluctuations that result from the changeable, early-winter weather.

In many bodies of water, that winter sanctuary is in deep water. The fall turnover which rejuvenated and mixed the lake's water also made the entire lake inhabitable for the bass. The area beneath the thermocline may have been virtually uninhabitable prior to the turnover, but now, with no thermocline and the mixing and cleansing of the water equalizing the oxygen content and temperature, the only unique thing about the extreme depths is that conditions there are more stable. The surface water layer acts as a buffer, and insulates the depths—and the fish that have taken up winter residence there—from weather-related changes that may be making the shallower reaches less hospitable to logy bass.

When the vast majority of the fish in any given body of water are gathered tightly into a few small areas, the rest of the lake, no matter how good it looks, offers little potential for the angler. Mechanical skills—casting ability, exceptional sense of feel—or temporary warming trends that might be expected to result in increased fish activity can do nothing to offset the absence of fish. To benefit from the congregating that the cold-water period brings, an angler must fish where the fish bunch up. That sounds so elementary, yet every winter it seems fishermen turn out in increased numbers when a warming trend occurs. "Fair-weather fishermen" rarely get in on the fall/winter action because their strategies are usually designed for the increased activity they expect to encounter rather than the seasonally mandated grouping. The areas in which bass congregate during the cold-water period are specifically insulated from changes in weather conditions, and their activity level does not reflect the weather conditions. In fact, they have absolutely no way of knowing that the shallows might be warming on any given day.

While it might seem that the entire deep basin area of a natural lake or main channel of a man-made impoundment would offer comparable conditions to winter bass that are concerned primarily with avoiding variations in water quality or temperature, that is rarely the case. Their tendency is to avoid organic bottoms which continue to consume oxygen through the winter. Once the water temperature reaches 39 degrees, convection ceases, and winter stratification begins, trapping the bottom waters once again. Rock and gravel areas in deep water are much more hospitable than silty bottoms.

Rock and gravel areas in deep water are not particularly common in many natural lakes, or in older reservoirs for that matter. Those that exist become extremely crowded with bass and other fish. In the absence of such areas or other environmentally stable options, deep suspension may be a fact of life.

The most notable environmentally stable condition other than depth is a submerged spring which releases a constant flow or seepage of water that is also constant in both temperature and chemistry. In some lakes—particularly shallow natural lakes—submerged springs are the primary sites of winter aggregation.

There are numerous clues to the presence of underwater springs, but they are certainly not as easy to identify as deep, hard-bottomed areas. For that reason, it's important to not only be aware of the various clues, but to make note of them when you find them and to then check them periodically when appropriate. Discovery of these springs may be circumstantial so you may not think to make note of their locations.

In latitudes where lakes ice over in winter, spring holes may be found simply because they are among the last spots on the lake to freeze over. In early to mid-fall, when dense, early-morning fog is commonplace, the location of spring holes may be revealed by "holes" in the fog layer. Conversely, on mornings without fog, those same spring holes might be given away by a cloud of heavy mist over the surface. Remember, the fog is created by the relationship between water temperature and the chill night air. Because the temperature of the area surrounding the spring is slightly different, the presence or lack of fog over a spot can be an important clue.

8

Cover

Structure fishing as a designation began to get widespread acceptance in the fishing community in the late '60s—especially in the bass fishing community. However, it's in the bass fishing world that the original definition of the word *structure* has changed. Among bass fishermen, structure has come to be used interchangeably with cover.

The two terms actually have very little in common. Structure is a recognizable place in the lake—usually on the lake floor—where the relationship between deep water and shallow is unique. Cover is someplace that bass or their prey can hide.

Cover can be an element of structure, but it isn't necessarily structure itself. To best realize this, consider a shallow, weed-choked, dishpan lake. A dense milfoil bed grows from one shoreline to the other. Plenty of cover. But that cover isn't structure. There are no landmarks, signposts or unique features of any kind for the bass to relate to. A weed-free spot a few dozen yards across could serve as structure in this environment.

Structure and cover both play important roles in bass life, and in some—perhaps most—situations, certain cover elements are integral to the structural makeup of a body of water. But a "naked" point extending out from a shoreline flat into a lake's deeper basin, while not having any cover on it, can also be structure.

Structure and cover are both important to bass. Structure that contains cover is usually more attractive to bass than structure that doesn't. Depending upon its layout and relationship to sur-

Anglers should watch for overhead cover—especially areas of broken cover or edges of cover—which offers adult largemouths a notable ambush-feeding advantage over their preyfish.

rounding conditions, cover can qualify as structure. This type of cover will hold more bass more often than cover that offers nothing more than a hiding place.

Role Of Overhead Cover/Shade

It is no secret that bass show a need to be near something. In reality, the entire premise of structure fishing is based on the fact that bass rarely sit in the middle of nowhere. They associate with objects—bottom irregularities, bottom composition changes. It's also widely recognized that bass—particularly largemouth bass— seem to have some ingrained need to relate to overhead cover, at least some of the time. Long ago, most anglers believed that because bass lack eyelids, sunlight hurt their eyes, and light-blocking, overhead cover offered a degree of protection. That theory was debunked. Nevertheless, bass do use overhead cover, and there must be some reason.

To understand the largemouth's special relationship with overhead cover, look no further than its predatory nature and unique role as a universal, non-discriminatory predator. Most fish are not equipped to utilize the feeding advantage that overhead cover provides; however, the largemouth bass is one of the few that can easily take a meal. Largemouths are not the fastest of fish; nor the most maneuverable. Compared to open-water species like salmon and stripers, it is quite easy for prey to outrun the bass. And most prey species take advantage of maneuvering in tight places that bass cannot enter. However, the bass does have effective camouflage. That camouflage is made even more effective by the shade and broken light patterns found in areas of overhead cover. A largemouth's excellent eyesight is an advantage that is maximized by the contrast between water exposed to sunlight and strong shade or overhead cover. A bass lying in cover can see prey while escaping detection.

Most important, it's got that mouth! Every bass fisherman should find an opportunity to observe and study adult bass in a tank. Watching one feed is truly an eye-opening experience. It rarely "bites," and almost never just swims up to something and closes its mouth on it—at least not if it's reasonably sure it's food. Instead, it opens that mouth, distends the lower portion of its throat and flares its gills, creating a sudden gush of current that leads directly into its throat. A minnow swimming within a foot or two of a bass that's ready to eat is moments away from being turned into a memory and a cloud of scales. There is little more than a blur as the bass pivots into head-on striking position and sucks in the minnow (and often some weeds or debris) without actually swimming any closer to it.

Many aspects of the physical makeup of a bass contribute to this feeding routine, but it's the mouth that makes it work. Smallmouths and spotted bass can suck in their prey in a similar fashion, but their success ratio is nowhere near the largemouth's except if the prey is rather small or the bass are within a few inches of their intended victim. A decent-sized largemouth, on the other hand, can and will make a 6-inch perch disappear even though the two fish are a foot apart. In the real world, the ambush along the edges of overhead cover is the advantage of this feeding style for bass.

Of course, cover generally is the land of feeding opportunity. Many prey species are not at home in open water. Instead, they spend their lives weaving through the submerged mazes that cover offers. This includes a wide variety of baitfish species, juvenile panfish and even young-of-the-year bass. It also includes crayfish, frogs and an assortment of incidentally encountered potential meals. In other words, in and around cover is often one of the best places for a bass to feed.

In deeper water, the relationship between the largemouth and overhead cover isn't as strong. The ambush advantage depends upon direct sunlight. In reduced or low-light situations, the use of that competitive advantage diminishes, as does the bass' use of overhead cover. At night, under very cloudy skies or in deeper water, the largemouth doesn't use overhead cover nearly as often as it does in shallow water in bright sunlight. In fact, overhead cover in deep water is often just a resting place for inactive bass.

This greatly affects the way anglers fish cover. In shallow water, overhead cover is important because it's used by feeding bass which are the easiest to catch. Beyond the depth to which sunlight penetrates, the importance of overhead cover reverses. Instead of cover being the target of efforts, as in shallower water, it now becomes a likely place to find the bass that may be more difficult to catch.

Numerous forms of cover exist in bass waters across the country. In different waters, the importance of each type of cover varies according to how structurally significant it is, as well as the total mix of cover and the prey species/habitat options presented in each body of water.

Vegetation As Cover

To some lake users, all vegetation is "seaweed." The non-fishing public can think in terms like that, but bass anglers need to know considerably more about the different types of aquatic vegetation in productive waters. Vegetation plays an extremely important role in the quarry's life.

Aquatic vegetation can be divided into three general categories: submergent (totally underwater), emergent (rooted underwater but protruding above the surface) and floating leaf (rooted underwater with stems rising to the surface and leaves floating on the surface). Of these three types, floating leaf and emergent vegetation probably receive the most attention from bass fishermen. However, submergent vegetation may play the most important role in the lives of many bass. To a certain extent, that's because weeds that are visible above the surface are more obvious. What self-respecting bass angler can resist tossing a few casts to a field of floating lily pads? Once involved, all it takes for the angler is a boil or two on the surface, and he's most likely in for a long stay.

But, there are pads, and there are pads. Different varieties of lily-pad species, along with other weed types like water chestnut that provide habitat conditions very similar to lily pads, offer different habitat options. The light patterns breaking through the overhead cover in a field of small, "dollar" pads, for instance, are very different than those in a bed of "elephant ear" pads. The difference does not seem particularly significant; however, because it offers a different level and complexity of camouflaging light variations, it might be more beneficial to one particular species of prey or another. (And NAFC Members already know how important prey is to bass.)

Coontail and milfoil-type weeds—filament-like leaves—offer different habitat conditions at different points in the season. It depends upon whether they have reached the surface, and if so, whether they have begun to mat over. In the latter case, they offer overhead protection that is not all that different from lily pads. Even in the case of those just reaching the surface, the cover is typically much thicker near the surface than near the bottom.

Here's a situation where there is a shore-to-shore expanse of visible pads and weeds. Obviously there is plenty of cover, but it's still a job to find the exact location of the bass.

Plants thrive in sunlight. The closer they grow toward the surface, the more luxuriant the growth becomes. The more lush the vegetation, the less light that can penetrate through the upper leaves. Thus, the lower sections of the plants become sparse. Then bass can swim beneath the layer of thicker cover whether the plants reach the surface or not.

Most bass anglers associate weeds with largemouths, and largely ignore vegetation when fishing smallmouths. It's true that except for rather uncommon situations, smallmouths are not particularly attracted to lily pads and expansive, heavily matted milfoil or coontail beds. However, this is more a factor of their limited use of overhead cover than of an aversion to weeds. They do often prowl the edges of coontail, milfoil and pad beds, especially under low-light conditions when prey relying on that type of cover for protection is more likely to be found near it rather than in it. And smallmouths often use weedbeds of other types—without the dense layer of overhead cover—as their primary feeding grounds, especially in the case of pondweeds or cabbage.

Pondweeds and cabbage are the broadleaf styles of submerged vegetation. A number of plant types belong to the cabbage family. If you fish natural lakes, you know the importance of cabbage—or at least you should. With the adaptability traits of bass, almost all weeds are good for bass and bass fishing. However, if there is a perfect bass habitat existing somewhere in this world, some type of cabbage is most likely an integral part of it.

The common forms of cabbage—curly leaf, tobacco leaf and broadleaf pondweeds—grow on firm bottoms and seem to be particularly attractive to crayfish. The plants' stalks will reach to the surface by late summer, but the leafy portion does not mat over on the surface the way the filamentous weed-types so often do. Cabbage grows best in clear to moderately clear water, and will root to almost the deepest level of light penetration. Even in the thickest cabbage patches, bass find ample maneuvering room among the stalks. The leaf size and the density variations within a typical cabbage bed seem to create an area of uneven light patterns, making the bass' natural camouflage coloration even more effective. The sparser growth sections provide "hunting grounds" for active bass on the prowl for a meal. Meanwhile, the thicker patches offer ideal ambush conditions for slightly less-aggressive bass. And because it typically grows to the maximum depth for rooted vegetation, it's often found on that important edge between open water and cover.

Whether it is because cabbage is a perfect habitat for bass or cabbage happens to grow best where other conditions are perfect for bass is arguable. However, the fact remains that bass and cabbage are inseparable wherever they coexist.

Another type of weed that's very important, especially in the northern part of the country, is sand grass. This is a low-growing, brittle-stemmed, rooted algae that forms a carpet on the lake bottom. Various species of sand grass grow anywhere from less than 6 inches to several feet high, and most will grow in rather extreme depths. Sand grass is commonly found on offshore humps in northern natural lakes, and it is often thought of as being particularly attractive to smallmouths. Like most forms of algae, it is a

Bass Hangouts In Vegetation

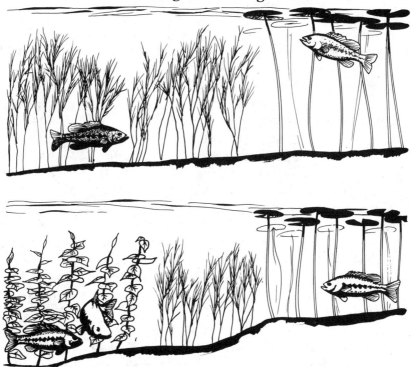

Different types of vegetation provide different cover densities, different prey and different habitat options. When these vegetation types meet, defined breaklines are formed which are very important to bass. The changes in the weedbeds often reflect changes in bottom depth or composition which is also important.

food source for crayfish. Thus, many crayfish live in sand grass carpets, making these carpets some of the most productive areas of any lake.

Whatever the type of weeds, density is an important factor in determining how frequently bass will use them. Variations in density are important. Remember, if it's all the same density it doesn't serve as structure, and density variations are what provide feeding opportunities. Some weed types, like cabbage, seem to grow naturally in varying density. Other weed types often grow as thick as possible, and variations within them occur only where bottom content changes or some object (like a submerged rock or stump) interrupts weed growth or where a different type of weed creates a variation.

Cover density variations create subtle edges. Abrupt edges

create a type of breakline known as a weed edge or weedline. It's simply the edge of the weed growth. Edges, of course, are the key areas along any form of habitat. The prototypical weedbed has at least two distinct edges. The outside weedline is formed in two ways. One is where the bottom drops below the level of sufficient light penetration for rooted weed growth to occur, and the other is in shallower lakes and impoundments where a silty bottom not conducive to rooted vegetation begins. The inside weedline is found along the bank (or other shallow areas where the bottom is at a too-shallow depth) or in areas that are unsuitable for the type of vegetation common to the lake.

Bare spots within the weedbed where, for one reason or another, the growth of the weedbed was interrupted also form weed edges. These are typically considered holes or pockets in the vegetation. Less distinct but often no less important weed edges are found where different types of vegetation meet. It is not unusual for a lake's vegetation to include numerous types of plant species, as well as distinct bands or zones within those species in the lake's littoral zone.

So, a lake's vegetation is rarely uniform. However, because it's so important to the bass, serious anglers should take the time to learn the nuances and intricacies of the weed-growth patterns in any lake they fish.

Shallow, protected areas with a soft bottom might support dense beds of small-leaf lily pads, while shallow areas over a harder bottom could feature large-leaf pads or reeds. Outside the reeds could be a strip of clean bottom which separates the reeds from a cabbage bed that extends out to the drop-off. Similarly, the area adjacent to the protected pads could hold milfoil or coontail which might extend all the way to the drop-off or might meet the outside cabbage. There could be a carpet of low-growing sand grass in an area where the shoreline flat extends out beyond the visible areas or on an underwater hump.

Any areas in which the relationship among several of those weed types is in some way different can be viewed as a spot where cover and structure coexist, and is most likely a high-percentage fishing spot. A narrower spot in the open-water band between the reeds and the cabbage, a "point" in the pad growth extending out into the coontail or a weed-free or sparsely vegetated rocky area along the edge where the cabbage and coontail meet are typical of the things that should grab an angler's attention while covering a weedbed. A condition like this anywhere within an otherwise-uniform weedbed is worth checking out. But when it occurs along a weedline—whether a major, outside or inside weedline or a weedline between two different weed types—it is an important feature.

In various parts of the country, other species of aquatic vegetation may take on added significance. In the Northeast, for instance, some waters—notably the Hudson River and Lake Champlain—support dense growths of water chestnut. Chestnut can be an extremely important habitat option for bass, but it can give fishermen nightmares. This is a floating leaf plant that seems incredibly hardy in midsummer but disappears quickly when the water starts to cool in the fall. Early in the summer, when the carpet of leaves on top of the water is only one layer thick, it fishes much like lily pads. By midsummer, though, the layer of vegetation may be 6 inches thick, with almost no holes or pockets to drop a lure into. Hundreds of acres of unbroken chestnut beds allow bass a sanctuary from all but the most determined fishermen.

Electric motors are useless in chestnut. The only chestnut-proof propulsion system is a push-pole. Hit a bed of chestnut with a bass boat that is running wide open and you might get 30 or so yards into it before being stopped, but don't expect to get out of it easily.

In the South, it's hydrilla and water hyacinth. Or arrowhead and sawgrass in Florida. In the upper Midwest, reeds are prevalent. Swiftly flowing rivers across much of the North support eel grass. All of these vegetation types have unique properties, but they all have certain things in common, as well. They all produce oxygen and provide some degree of cover. They all hold prey, and some provide excellent ambush positions for the opportunistic largemouth. Any aquatic vegetation is worth investigating, but the edges and especially the irregularities in those edges are the key factors. The less uniform a vegetation bed is, whether it's because of irregular bottom contour or composition or the presence of other types of weeds and cover, the more likely it is to be holding bass.

Rocks

In some sections of the country, rocks are abundant in bass

waters, while in others they are not often encountered. Although rocks are traditionally thought of as being more important to smallmouths than to largemouth bass, that belief may be proved false. A Canadian-Shield situation may exist: a matter of smallmouths being the more common species in geographical areas where rocks are the predominant bottom material. Where both largemouths and smallmouths coexist in rocky waters, both species use the rocks. In areas where cover offered by rocks doesn't lend itself to ambush feeding methods, that aspect of the largemouth's lifestyle doesn't typically come into play.

Spotted bass, too, use rocks, especially those associated with steep drop-offs. Steep drop-offs are important, at least on a seasonal basis, wherever they occur. Bluff banks are typically formed of rock, as are many well-defined underwater drop-offs. Spotted bass use these areas throughout the summer and fall, and largemouth often congregate in front of bluff banks in the winter. Rocky areas are important in winter for another reason. Popular post-turnover gathering places for bass are usually spots where there is minimal decaying organic material on the bottom, consuming oxygen and diminishing the overall water quality. This makes rocky bottoms, in many bass waters, the best option available to fish that are settling in for the winter.

Sheer rock faces—whether horizontal or vertical—offer little to the bass. It's not so much the rocks that are important as the cracks and crevices between them. In some situations, those nooks and crannies act as cover for the bass, but more frequently, they provide homes for the preyfish and crayfish that bass depend upon for food. The more uneven the rocks, the better their food-holding potential, and the more likely they are to be regularly visited by bass.

Riprap banks are man-made rock structure designed to retard erosion along seawalls and especially where roads are built adjacent to water. When they are adjacent to current, they can be the most productive. The uneven face of the riprap slows the flow of water next to it, creating numerous eddies and washes. Bass and baitfish find resting spots and feeding opportunities in the current breaks.

Wood

Among things that can draw a bass fisherman's attention, only

Nothing attracts a bass fisherman's attention like a fallen tree. He will often find bass—particularly largemouths—hanging out under the trunk and around the submerged branches.

a handful are in a league with a partially submerged tree, log or stump. Like a bed of lily pads, or a school of bass chasing bait on the surface, visible wood demands attention. It's not that totally submerged wood is less likely to hold fish—with one notable exception. It's just that it's more likely to go unnoticed.

The exception is in early spring when wood has been in the water for a long time. Early in the season, wood that breaks the water's surface warms more quickly from solar radiation than wood that's completely submerged—especially wood that is so deep it's not easily seen. But wood that's been submerged a while typically is covered with algae, making it home to all sorts of microscopic and nearly microscopic life forms. These life forms that live in and on shallower wood are triggered into activity much sooner than those residing on deeply submerged wood. Small fish encountering this confined area of activity find themselves in an unseasonably early feeding situation, and take up residence along that wood. Wandering bass also find this kind of feeding opportunity advantageous so they too are likely to hang around.

Fallen trees along the bank are perhaps the most common form of wooden cover because they are found in impoundments, natural lakes, ponds, rivers and streams. Most other forms of wood cover are limited to impoundments and rivers. When a tree near the water's edge falls, it usually falls into the water because its root network nearest the water is more likely to have been washed away.

Because bass are around banks so often, it doesn't take them long to discover a newly fallen tree. If that tree has leaves, their decay will add to the fertility, and attract more life forms sooner even though the leaves are not necessarily attractive to bass. In fact, the needles of some evergreen trees—notably hemlock—seem to dissuade bass from using the area until the needles have rotted away.

A deadfall in the back end of a shallow bay is cover, and will be used by fish if fish use the area at all. The same tree in the water on a steeper bank, however, is not only cover, but structure as well. It not only provides a fertile environment for lower life forms, hiding cover for baitfish and possible ambush cover for largemouths, but it serves as a bridge to the deeper water from the bank in a way that is unique compared to the adjacent bank. Bass magnet!

A single tree or log in the water along a fairly steep bank is an automatic. It's a spot you must check. A bank lined with fallen trees, though, may not be as attractive. It doesn't have that unique relationship between the depths and the bank. Fish will use it, and at times it could be chock full of bass. However, it's not the high-percentage target that the single tree is.

Along many such timber-strewn banks, one tree might be the key to bass moving onto the bank regularly. It might be the largest, or the one with the thickest tangle of branches; however, it's most likely the location of where it fell. The underlying structural configuration of the bottom is no less important just because of the presence of all that cover. Anglers must learn to see more than the obvious cover when searching for the areas fish use.

Submerged and partially submerged stumps are as attractive to

If one type of cover is good, several could certainly be better! Bass find conditions particularly suitable where several different types of structure are found mixed together, such as when wood and rocks are found together.

bass as any other form of cover. This is especially true in the case of stumps that grow along a depth break. Erosion often washes out the soil on the deep side of the stump in such situations. This results in a spot that not only offers the natural appeal of the stump itself, but provides overhead cover amidst the tangle of roots.

Similarly, shallow stumps in reservoirs and in natural lakes where the water levels have been raised artificially often have holes within the root network; the stump's natural flotation tries to lift it toward the surface while wave action works on the topsoil surrounding the stump. Although not as attractive year-round as stumps located on a drop-off, this stump situation can be particularly important in the springtime. Depending on its specific layout, the stump may be used as a staging area for females, or bass might bed under it, on top of it, or in the junctures of the roots themselves. It can be a critical piece of cover.

With the impoundment construction boom of the '60s a fading memory, standing timber in reservoirs is becoming more a memory than an important factor in bass-fishing strategies. Still, where flooded timber remains, it is a major consideration. Just as in the case discussed earlier, areas loaded with standing timber should be considered cover rather than structure.

The relationship between deep and shallow water and how the cover configuration relates to that is of primary importance. In older impoundments where much of the wood has fallen, the horizontal pieces—especially the thicker horizontals—are more important than the standing trees themselves, unless they've fallen in water so deep that they're out of the depth range regularly used by bass.

Submerged treetops that are existing 10 to 30 feet beneath the surface can be extremely important factors in finding bass in midsummer. Although there may be another 40 or 50 feet of water beneath the treetops, these areas function much in the manner of underwater humps. They provide something for bass to relate to in the middle of nowhere. They disrupt the normal migration patterns of shad, creating a prime feeding opportunity for predators like bass.

Brush and bushes in the water take on a seasonal importance when spring flood waters expand the boundaries of a lake. Baitfish and panfish often push back into the flooded brush, and the bass follow. In this situation, water is typically muddy, and thick brush can act much like weeds in filtering the water.

Bass that move back into flooded brush in the spring are typically very nervous. *Nervous* is, of course, not quite an accurate word here because it suggests an emotion that bass don't actually possess. However, in this case, it describes the tendency of bass to leave brush at the first sign of receding water levels.

In fishing this situation, watch for areas where the water funnels through as the lake level returns to normal. Baitfish and assorted terrestrial forage will wash through these funnels, and ever-opportunistic bass will stack up in front of these funnels for some windfall feeding.

Not all wood enters the water by way of nature. Docks, piers, seawalls and other assorted man-made constructions hold their share of bass as well. The usual considerations about the impor-

Docks and bass go together. Of course, not all docks are great spots for bass fishing; however, some can be super fishing spots. This type of dock had all the credentials.

tance of the bottom structure configuration relating to specific wooden cover, of course, apply. But there are several general rules regarding man-made wooden structure that can help you identify those with the greatest potential for holding fish:

(a) Permanent docks, attached to the bottom, are better than floating docks.

(b) Old and dilapidated is better than new.

(c) Complex docks (L- or T-shaped) are better than simple (square or straight) docks.

(d) Docks with horizontal or angular cross-members are far more productive than those without these features. (And the heavier the horizontal members, the better.)

(e) The closer to the water's surface the dock lies, the better.

(f) Docks with a chair or two and perhaps a few rod holders

Wood pilings—especially if they've been in the water a long time, as have these—develop algae coats that become small aquatic communities, supporting a number of different life forms. This kind of activity attracts bass and should attract anglers.

mounted on them are likely to have a brush pile or other "added incentives" nearby.

Items (a), (c), (d) and, to a certain extent, (f) all stem from the fact that the more wood in the water at any specific dock or pier, the better the situation for bass that might be using the structure. Item (f) has the additional attraction of an unseen section that reaches into deeper water, making the dock more structurally significant (as opposed to being merely a form of cover).

Item (b) is related to the fact that wood submerged for a longer period naturally has a greater algae buildup on it, and supports a wider diversity of life forms. In this regard, many newer docks are built with pressure-treated lumber, which not only resists algae buildup, but may actually repel bass because of the arsenic permeating the water.

Item (e) is important primarily because of the more effective shade-producing capabilities of something that lies close to the water's surface. The shade is always underneath it, rather than moving with the sun through the course of the day, as is the case with docks that tower above the water's surface. A secondary benefit is that large, low-lying docks, especially those with lots of timbers reaching into the water, are difficult for most anglers to fish, other than just by skimming the outside edges. That means they have a greater chance of holding bass that have not been hooked or caught frequently. It's often worth the time, effort and aggravation to get a lure far back underneath such docks.

Weeds, wood, rocks: All of these things represent cover, and all come in a wide variety of types. The greater the diversity in any habitat, the more potentially productive, bass-catching patterns exist. Developing a system of checking cover quickly and efficiently is a major step toward advanced bass-fishing success; however, this does not mean fishing fast—a topic which will be discussed in later chapters on activity levels and position/location.

9

Where Habitats Meet

Break and breakline, like structure, are terms that have been so widely used, overused and misused in the context of fishing over the past 20 years that the original meaning seems to have been lost in the shuffle. Just as structure is more than cover, a breakline is more than a drop-off. But if the word encompasses more than the obvious drop-off, what exactly does it include?

Breaklines are many things to many people, depending on the bodies of waters that they fish. To many reservoir-bred anglers, breakline means the edge of a creek channel. A natural-lake fisherman might think in terms of the deep edge of the weed growth, and a river-rat might look to current shear lines or mudlines as the important keys to bass location. All these examples are, of course, breaklines. What is really important, however, is what they are to the bass.

Perhaps the best definition is "the edge created where two different habitats meet." This definition includes all the obvious breaklines. It's easy to see that an impoundment's channel edge (where the shallow to mid-depth flat drops off into the deep water of the old creek bed) is a breakline. Or the deep-water edge of the shoreline-related weedbeds in a natural lake which marks the boundary between the cover-laden, food-producing littoral zone and the open water of the basin. The fast current edge in a riverine situation is equally important.

This definition also includes the breaklines that are not quite

Changes in the shape of this shoreline, like this small pocket, should draw the attention of any serious bass angler. Also important to the fish (but less obvious to the angler) are changes in submerged breaklines.

Where Habitats Meet

When Bass Have Confinement Advantage

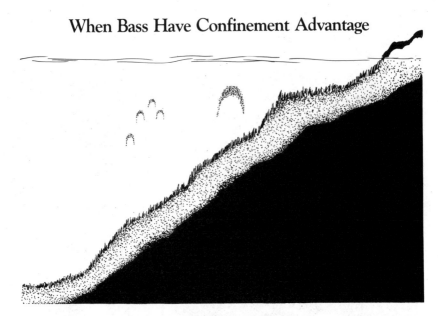

The confinement advantage bass (small symbols) have when trapping a school of baitfish (large symbol) against the shoreline is pronounced. As the school disperses, those shad forced onto the shallow flat have no way to escape, and become a tasty meal for the bass.

so "cut and dried:" edges like the one formed where a lily-pad bed meets a lush growth of coontail, or where dingy water meets clear, warm water abuts cool or a sand/gravel bottom changes to silt and muck. Breaklines in this mold may be less obvious, but they are not necessarily less significant than the major drop-offs that come to mind when the word *breakline* is freely tossed about in bass-fishing circles.

"Major" breaklines dominate fishing strategies because they often represent the edge of the bass' territory, as opposed to simply an edge between two acceptable but different territories. Perhaps the most important breakline in any body of water isn't the structure-oriented angler's favorite drop-off or the deep wedge of the weed growth that so many natural-lake bass experts key on but the breakline that first drew the attention of bass anglers—the shoreline. While anglers who have learned all about structure fishing have steered clear of the shoreline, it's no coincidence that bass have been caught for generations by anglers casting to the bank. It's simply the most important breakline in the lake. It's the edge where an inhabitable environment for bass abruptly meets one in which they cannot exist.

Never underestimate the bass-holding potential of the shoreline. To predatory bass, the most important breaklines may be those that define the edges of the habitat their prey occupies. The shoreline obviously meets that requirement in a great many cases, with both aquatic and terrestrial life-forms in abundance. Bass often trap baitfish against the bank. By eliminating at least one potential escape path, the shallow shelf along the shoreline gives the bass that is not otherwise particularly adept at open-water pursuit an advantage. And to the opportunistic bass, a potential victim falling into its world from terra firma is a windfall feeding opportunity. Whether it's a mouse, a caterpillar or an earthworm, it doesn't matter to the bass. It's alive; it's obviously struggling as it tries to make its way back to its own environment, and it's within edible size range. That's all it usually takes to convince an active bass to take a chance.

Break-On-A-Breakline And Intersecting Breaklines

Just as a breakline is where bottom and/or water conditions change, the spot where the breakline conditions change is the break-on-a-breakline. Like breaklines, they can be obvious and well-defined—like a boulder along the edge of a weedbed or a pronounced corner on the edge of a shoreline-related shelf. Or they can be subtle like a slot of slightly deeper water crossing the edge of a weedline or a single log lying horizontally along the edge of a stand of submerged timber that consists of mostly standing trees. These kinds of changes are often difficult to find.

Whatever it is, it's different from the rest of the breakline (or at least from the breakline stretches adjacent to it on either side). Any break might hold a fish, but one located on or adjacent to a breakline is more likely to hold fish more often. Therefore, it's a high-percentage fishing spot.

The end of a point is a turn in the breakline formed by the point and a commonly fished break-on-a-breakline. But what about the spot where the drop-off meets the shoreline shelf? This inside turn could hold more fish more often than the obvious, outside turn at the end of the point. While this subject will be discussed later during a look at the relationship between a fish's activity level and its position, keep in mind that breaks-on-breaklines do not need to be objects, like boulders, or cover such as bushes, to be important to the bass. Turns in the breakline offer-

Bass anglers who are schooled in the structure-fishing discipline often overlook the fact that the shoreline actually is the ultimate breakline. It's the edge of inhabitable territory for fish.

ing something extra, like an advantage over prey or some other aspect of a bass' normal behavior pattern, are especially attractive to bass.

Fairly sharp turns in breaklines, such as those just discussed, are among the best fish-holding structure in any lake. This seems especially true with weed edges and drop-offs; however, that may be because turns in those types of breaklines are more obvious. A sharp turn in a breakline formed where one type of bottom meets another, for instance, is not nearly as easy to recognize. To the bass, however, it may be just as important.

Obvious corners are easy to find and recognize. Subtle ones, on the other hand, can be easily overlooked. It can be just a change in the makeup of the breakline, for example, like a drop-off that runs from a 10-foot-deep lip into 20 feet of water, and there's one small spot where the top edge extends out to 12 feet before dropping off. Not much of a change to an angler's eyes, but to the fish, it could be the prime location along a quarter-mile-long stretch of breakline!

Keeping in mind that the shoreline is the ultimate breakline, think of a log or stump along the bank as a break-on-a-breakline. Memories of all those bass you've caught casting to shallow, shoreline-related targets over the years will make it a lot easier to invest some time searching for breaks on not-so-obvious break-lines. Any change in conditions you might find along the bank— a small pocket or protrusion in the shoreline, a slightly steeper section of bank, a bush, rock or log—would automatically draw your attention and your efforts. Experience quickly teaches us that bass are object-oriented creatures. They are just as object-oriented when there is 15 feet of water between them and the surface and a long distance between them and the bank.

Would a change in bottom composition or a slight change in the shoreline's angle draw your attention as quickly as a stump or undercut along that bank? It should. And that same, less obvious break along a deeper and less easily examined breakline should be thoroughly investigated—by means of electronic aids (depth-finder or chart recorder) and by the braille method (feeling around it with a jig or other bottom-contact lure).

Subtle Breaklines And Breakbands

The structure-oriented bass angler typically places maximum emphasis on pronounced breaklines—steep drop-offs, sudden changes in bottom composition, clean weed edges. However, lakes lacking steep drops and pronounced weedlines hold bass, too. A lake bottom that dropped 3 feet in depth across a span of 30 or 40 feet would be a flat on many waters. On others, it could be the sharpest drop-off in the lake!

It wouldn't have to be the sharpest drop in the lake for bass to make use of it, of course. It would just have to provide them with something that surrounding areas didn't. That "something" usu-ally amounts to food.

While abrupt, distinct breaklines are most readily identified, two different habitats often merge rather than abut. Drop-offs can be moderately tapered; weeds often thin out as the water gets deeper, rather than ending in a well-defined "wall," and water

Among the many breaklines that bass anglers should work is the water-color breakline which is often overlooked. Although difficult to show here, this breakline is pronounced.

color or quality breaklines are often more a mixture of water from two areas rather than a distinct edge.

An advantage exists in fishing the more distinct breaklines. They help pinpoint the fish and narrow down the area to be checked with lures. There is no advantage, however, if the fish happen to be using an area where the breakline is less precisely formed. Check the easy breaklines first; but, don't ignore the breaklines that will be more time-consuming or difficult. You have to fish where the fish are, not where you'd like them to be.

Water-Color/Water-Quality Breaklines

Some of the fastest fishing an NAFC angler is likely to experience can be found along breaklines that might only exist for a few days. Mudlines or water-color breaklines are rarely permanent fixtures. Often, the conditions that create them also happen to induce a windfall feeding opportunity that bass and other predators capitalize on. Water-quality (oxygen/temperature/pH) breaklines are also possible, but nine times out of 10, they exist in conjunction with a water-color breakline. Something has to move a sizeable quantity of water to create this kind of breakline. The kinds of forces capable of this feat almost invariably cause turbulence that stirs up bottom mud, adding color to the mix. It's a good thing, too, because these things are difficult to fish even with the visual clue of a color change. Doing it by instrumentation alone could be a bass-fishing nightmare. It may be an advantage to find a different pattern to key on.

Water-temperature and oxygen-content breaklines without a telltale color line are a fact of life for Great Lakes salmon anglers who must contend with an extended period of strong winds—especially easterly or northeasterly winds—that can push surface water for miles, allowing colder water from below the thermocline to reach the surface. This isn't a turnover because the thermocline doesn't disintegrate or deteriorate, and the two water masses remain separate. But even these "temperature walls," which form on the lee side of the lake perhaps several miles from shore, are usually detected as a result of a "trash line" of accumulated floating debris along the thermal barrier preventing the waters from mixing. Such circumstances rarely affect bass and bass fishermen, but it should help them understand how strong an influence the wind can have on the water and how effective a barrier to circulation the thermocline can be. As far as bass fishing is concerned, however, they can usually expect to find a marked and notable water-color difference where a mass of water is being moved.

The three basic types of water-color breaklines that we should be aware of are wind driven, runoff driven and reverse runoff.

Wind-driven mudlines are the result of a strong and prolonged wind beating on one specific shoreline. The intensity of the created mudline is a matter of how much silt and soil there is on the shoreline flat. A predominantly rock and gravel shoreline might be in just as much turmoil; however, if there isn't much dirt to mix with the water, the water-color breakline that forms may not be very noticeable.

When the waves pound a shoreline, several things happen, and any or all of them can lead to increased fish activity along that bank. Plankton—the base of the food chain—is pushed against the shoreline. Open-water baitfish are either driven by the wind or follow the plankton. Not only is food more heavily concentrated in the area, but both the open-water baitfish and the resident prey species along the shallow shelf are buffeted about in the turbulence along the bank. Disoriented and struggling prey is easier to capture, and more powerful swimmers like bass take advantage of it.

If the wind isn't hitting the bank obliquely, it usually forms a current along the bank. This allows bass to hold in protected areas behind objects and feed in the current, much like river fish.

Another current is also formed in this situation, causing problems in interpreting wind-driven, water-color breaklines. As water is blown toward a bank, water that's already there must move to make way for it. While surface water is pushed against the bank, water nearer the bottom moves away from the bank, flowing out toward the lake basin. Bass often hold along the water-color breakline near the bottom, where the flow is bound away from shore. There, they pick off disoriented prey being washed out in the undertow.

The angler's problem is locating the breakline position. It is almost invariably outside its apparent position (where you seem to see the water-color line on the surface). Casting into the muddied water and allowing the current to wash the lure out from the bank is the key. You'll have to assist it along in most cases because the push on the line may negate the undertow's pull on your lure. Whatever you do, don't put your lure right on top of the visible water-color breakline; it won't be out where that breakline actually is located.

Runoff-driven mudlines are the result of heavy rains muddying feeder streams. Along with the soil, all sorts of stream resident forage and terrestrial life forms that were washed into the stream are pushed out into the lake or river by the runoff. Again, it's a windfall forage opportunity that bass take advantage of. The bass typically sit just outside the mudline and intercept the assorted prey that's being washed out into the lake.

Once again, the problem is locating the actual position of the mudline and the point at which the intense flow disperses at the depth the bass are at. The visual mudline is an inviting clue, but it can often be misleading. The best way to locate the position you

A man-made breakline (in this case, a stone wall) is another spot that bass anglers should consider. Note the intersection between the two walls. Could you find it and fish it effectively in 15 feet of water?

need to fish in this situation is to check the water temperature on both sides of the mudline. If the runoff is warmer than the lake water, it will ride along the surface, and the mudline 8 or 10 feet down might be far back underneath from where it appears to be from the surface. If the runoff is colder than the lake water, it will flow along the bottom. You may have to fish some distance out in apparently clean water in order to actually fish on the edge of the roiled runoff flow.

Reverse runoff water-color breaklines aren't caused by the lake water running back up into the stream but represent the tail end of muddied water flowing from the stream. This is not so much a breakline that fish relate to as it is a clue to the probable short-term location of a sizeable number of fish. This situation is common in mountainous areas where the predominant geological feature is rock. Streams clear quickly in those areas, because there is very little loose topsoil to wash away. Within several days of a heavy rainstorm, all the muddy runoff has been deposited in the lake, and the stream water is running clear.

Now, the mudline is on the opposite side, with the lake muddy and the stream mouth clear. In this situation, an angler

Where Habitats Meet   117 should get as far into the clear water as possible. Fish that live in a normally clean environment will only put up with grit in their gills for so long. When the heavy flow they have been keying on starts to clear up, they often swim directly into the clean water.

Man-Made Breaklines

In many waters, some of the most important breaklines are the result of man-made structure. Roadbeds, fences, stone walls and other man-made objects represent distinct breaklines to the fish. Spots where such breaklines meet, cross or simply happen to exist in conjunction with each other or with some natural breakline or cover can be extremely meaningful.

Roadbeds are often elevated from the surrounding country-side, and may parallel a drainage ditch. The resulting structural makeup of such an area when it's inundated can be an exceptional area for finding fish. Depending upon its depth and composition (Dirt roads are more productive than paved roads.), the road itself might serve the same function as a hump. The adjacent ditch offers a depth break that fish could retreat into under less-than-ideal weather and water conditions.

Unusual bottom configurations, especially when there are nooks and crannies for prey to hide in, are among the most used areas by deep-water bass. A ravine intersecting a roadbed at a right angle is often a clue that there is a culvert or pipe passing under the roadway. That culvert usually is surrounded by riprap. It would be difficult to find a much more ideal spot for bass to relate to even if it were designed specifically for the purpose. (Well, maybe some brush could be dumped into the ditch—a not-at-all uncommon condition in situations like this.)

Bridge abutments and causeways are other man-made breaks that bass anglers should not overlook. On rivers and impound-ments, current is a natural occurrence and, where it passes under a roadway or railroad trestle, is often particularly attractive to bass—for a number of reasons. Even on natural lakes, there are similar situations. Despite not having a riverbed, most natural lakes have some type of outflow. Unless a causeway or bridge cuts across a "dead water" bay with no inlet, there is usually some water flow through the passage.

Even the smallest causeways should be investigated. The natural effect of such a structure which concentrates the flow into one specific area is to magnify the strength of the current that flows through it. The downstream corners of the opening create eddies, and are often key holding areas for feeding fish. The corners on the opposite side of the road often act as "snags" where floating timber or brush get hung up, creating yet another potential fish-holding spot.

Causeway culverts are typically "one fish" spots. Bridge abutments, on the other hand, can be the kind of place where you can spend the day fishing. Not that they necessarily are, but they do have the potential.

Economics dictate that bridges be built in the narrowest and/or shallowest positions on any given stretch of water. Eddies form any place that the speed of the water movement changes. Eddies and current-living bass go hand in hand. If a bridge is a part of a causeway, as is so often the case on flatland-style reservoirs, this current multiplying effect and the eddies associated with it are compounded. These abutments can be major feeding areas for all bass species; but, spotted bass, smallmouths and the lesser species are prone to use major bridge abutments more than sizeable largemouths. And, bridge abutments rising from a bottom within the depth range used regularly by bass are much more productive than those that come up out of 40 or 50 feet of water.

Aggressively feeding fish also are more often attracted to the smaller pocket of still water and the almost whirlpool-like eddies that often form on the upstream face and corners of the bridge abutment.

10

Bass Environments

akes not dug or impounded by man are actually natural lakes. These freshwater bodies include everything from small potholes to Florida's Lake Okeechobee and the Great Lakes. And, except for far northern Canada and Alaska, it's difficult to find one in North America in which there aren't one or more species of thriving bass. Because the complexity of any aquatic environment tends to be directly proportional to its size, it may be best to categorize smaller natural lakes—under 150 to 200 acres—as ponds as well as natural lakes because they share certain traits with both.

Nature has used various forces to create natural lakes. Some—Reelfoot in Tennessee and Champlain on the Vermont/New York border, for instance—owe their existence to earthquakes. Oxbow lakes are, in essence, natural lakes formed by meandering rivers. But most of the natural lakes in North America—and the ones that will be discussed here—were formed by glaciers.

As the glaciers pushed their way southward during the last ice age, they scoured holes and depressions in the earth's surface, pushing glacial till ahead of their paths. As these glaciers receded, water from the melting ice and snow filled these depressions, and lakes were born.

Because these glaciers retreated to the north, the oldest natural lakes are the most southerly, and were created thousands of years before the youngest of the glacial lakes in the far-northern reaches of Canada. The age of a lake is important because the en-

While recognizing the importance of the primary food shelf and vegetation in natural lakes, anglers should remember that a hard-bottomed rise beyond the weed-growth edge can possibly hold a large number of bass.

Bass Environments

vironment within it evolves as the aging process occurs.

The typical glacially formed lake started as a deep, steep-sided gouge in the earth's crust. Its basin started at its shoreline, and the bottom composition was primarily rock. Over the first few dozen centuries of the lake's existence, the annual freeze-and-thaw cycle of the surface waters continually fractured rock along the shoreline and thousands of years of wind and wave erosion further wore into the banks, creating the shoreline shelves that play such a major role in the lives of resident bass.

As erosion continued, smaller particles settled into the deep basin, making the basin shallower. Eventually, simple life-forms took up residence in the lake. Living creatures produce organic waste, and they die, becoming organic waste themselves.

As organic waste accumulated, primarily in the basin silt and in protected shallow areas around the expanding shoreline shelf, the lake's overall fertility level increased, paving the way for more life-forms—both biological and botanical. As organic materials became ingrained in the sand, gravel and the shoreline shelf's marl, enough bottom fertility became available to support rooted vegetation. Eventually, all that was left of the lake's original floor was the lip of the major drop-off, from the eroded flat to the now-silted basin. At some point in the lake's life, fertility results in increased siltation at a rate sufficient enough to fill the basin to a point that the lip all but disappears. From this point on, advancing eutrophication (aging process) overtakes the lake, and it literally starts to die. Continued siltation makes the lake shallower and smaller until it eventually becomes more of a swamp than a lake. One day, it will be dry land again.

Of course, all this doesn't take place in a span of time that humans can easily comprehend. But it's undeniable that the presence of civilization near a lake speeds up the process. As land in the watershed is developed, erosion patterns change, accelerating externally originated siltation. The nutrients humans create—both by their own biological functions and the artificially induced fertilizers used on lawns of lakefront homes and on farmlands—eventually leach into the lake, further raising the water's fertility level and the basin—and accelerating the siltation process.

The Food Shelf
Most of the forage in natural lakes is produced in, and stays in,

the littoral zone. If you define the littoral zone as the area of the lake in which sunlight penetrates to the bottom, you won't be far off. If water were of uniform clarity, that would be twice the depth to which you could maintain visual contact with a white object lowered into the water. (Limnologists use something called a secchi disk, but for anglers' purposes, a white-skirted spinnerbait works just fine). In practice, light penetration and, correspondingly, the littoral zone extend somewhat deeper than twice the level at which you can still see that object because the light you're looking at has passed through any layers of suspended particulates twice: once on the way down, and once after it's been reflected off the object you're looking at.

That littoral zone is the food shelf. It extends from the lake's shoreline to at least the first major break, but never beyond the depth of light penetration. If the shoreline shelf extends for a long distance beyond the maximum depth of light penetration before reaching the break into the basin, the extended shelf may be used by bass, but not as heavily as the shallower reaches. Bass don't need sunlight, at least not all the time. However, botanical life-forms do. The most active portions of any body of water are those where there is a balance between the botanical and the biological life-forms.

The Basin

The basin area is simply the deep, open-water section of the lake. In all but the purely oligotrophic lakes in the far northern reaches of the continent, the basin's bottom is composed primarily of a mixture of decaying organic compounds and finely ground particles of soil.

When considering a natural lake's basin area, anglers often think of the thermocline, and bass-fishing experts have long held that bass do not travel beneath the thermocline. That is not always the case. In relatively infertile environments, the water trapped beneath the thermocline can have the same oxygen content as the water above it. In such an environment, there is little decay, and the creatures living in the extreme depths operate at subdued metabolic rates consuming little oxygen. The dissolved oxygen in the water beneath the thermocline can last through the summer.

Of course, this means that bass living in such an environment

The presence of reeds in a lake should alert anglers. These reeds are a common form of bass habitat in natural lakes across much of the country.

are free to use the basin. If and when they do, it would be as a stress response from a probable food scarcity. (If the lake is that infertile, this is a very real possibility).

It is important to realize that while the offshore humps may rise from the basin, there are very often less notable hard-bottomed rises protruding through the layer of silt as well. These spots may take on considerable significance in the cold- water period when bass often retreat to the depths to find relief from unsteady environmental conditions in the shallower reaches. This is area where they spend a lot of time during warmer seasons, too.

The Primary Break

The primary break is simply the first notable drop-off from the shoreline shelf into or toward the basin. It's actually the major remnant of part of the original lake foundation. Variations in the primary break and accordingly in the shoreline shelf are what constitute the structural configuration of a natural lake. Areas where it's steeper or less steep represent places where a unique relationship between the shallow shelf and the depths of the basin exist. Places where the breakline juts out toward the center of the basin from points on the littoral flat, and areas where a secondary shelf interrupts the drop into the basin, providing a suitable deep-water habitat for fish and larval insect life that fish feed upon.

Weeds, Weed Edges Are Important

Although the geological/topographical configuration of natural lakes is important in the overwhelming majority of bass-holding natural lakes in the U.S., and a good number of the "younger" lakes in Canada, it's the lake's flora content that deserves the credit for most of the population, and, therefore, most of the fishing opportunity.

The outside (deep-water) edge of the weed growth and the primary breakline form twin pivot points in gamefish movements. Each represents a break from one habitat to another. Perhaps the most important aspect of a glacial lake's makeup, then, is the relationship between these two important features.

The presence or lack of a lip between the two defines much about the way bass use the area. Spots where the two features meet, with no relatively flat lip extending beyond the weed growth, fit very differently into the activity of bass than do spots where such a lip does exist. When checking for "outside" bass on a natural lake, be sure to note whether they are taken on "lipped" sections of the weed edge or in places where the weed edge meets the primary break and drops directly into deeper water.

11

Impoundments

I mpoundment and reservoir are terms that can both be used to describe bodies of water created by man rather than nature. In some areas of the country, however, the word *reservoir* implies an impoundment built specifically for the purpose of storing drinking water. To avoid confusion, only the word *impoundment* will be used here. This discussion will be limited to impoundments created by the construction of a dam across a river valley.

Man-made bodies of water such as strip pits and gravel mines are technically impoundments as well, but their small size and the lack of a pronounced creek channel keeps them from functioning in the manner typical of impoundments. Therefore, they will be covered in the chapter on ponds.

Make no mistake about it, nature does a much better job of creating bodies of water than does man. Glacial lakes started their life as sterile gouges in the earth's surface, with only incidental occurrences of organic matter within their borders, and evolved over thousands of years into the living ecosystems that support bass today. Impoundments, on the other hand, begin their lives with a basin that is already fertile, and are thus destined to have a much shorter life span than natural lakes.

Other features that distinguish impoundments from natural lakes are the pronounced creek channel, the volume of water flowing through the impoundment and the presence of non-natural and non-aquatic properties. Some impoundments were

The deep, clear impoundments of the West offer different challenges for the serious bass angler who is accustomed to the murkier natural lakes and ponds found in other parts of the country.

Impoundments

bulldozed before being flooded, wiping away most traces of man's presence on what was to be the bottom, and most signs of wood as well. But in most, old roadbeds, fences, stone walls, house foundations, bridges and other assorted features carried over from the previous landscape exist, as does the stumpage of former forested land and, in many cases, extensive stands of timber.

All these things provide an environment with unique spots for bass and usually a greater diversity of potential cover. Most impoundments also have at least one section where the habitat is more river-like than lake-like. All told, impoundments typically offer more varied habitat options to bass than do most natural lakes or rivers.

Basic Impoundment Types

While it's possible to divide impoundments into several categories, doing so makes the entire process too complicated, so they will be divided into two very broad types. The types are those where the drop into the creek channel is at a usable (by bass) depth, and those where the drop is out of the normal depth range for bass.

Flatland, lowland or midland impoundments fall into the first category. The shoreline drop might be a gradual slope or a reasonably steep drop into the mid-depths, and the flat area between the shoreline or the shoreline's base drop and the edge of the creek channel is potential bass territory. In shallower versions of this type of impoundment, the main river channel is often less than 30 feet deep.

The majority of highland impoundments, the cavernous impoundments typical of the Western U. S., along with some of the deepest, hilly land impoundments, fit into the latter category.

The effective difference between these two broad types is that in the deep-channel variety, most bass activity for most of the year is found within a long cast of the shoreline, while on flatter reservoirs, shorelines of coves, bays and inlets are important in spring and possibly in early fall (especially the back ends of major creek arms) but may be used only incidentally during the summer and winter. Offshore structure, especially relating to the main channel and its confluences with side channels, become key areas in winter and summer in much the same way as the primary break and outside weedline in a glacially formed lake.

If an angler moves far enough upstream in almost any impoundment, he'll find riverine conditions and bass acting more like river bass than lake bass.

As indicated earlier, wood cover is common in many impoundments. For most, it's stumps, while in some impoundments, standing timber remains from when the impoundment was filled. In the early days of those impoundments, almost all fishing efforts revolved around the timber. As more and more of that wood decays, though, and as the impoundments mature from newly formed fisheries filled with cover and nutrients to balanced ecosystems, the wood loses more and more of its importance in fish movements.

Vegetation's Importance In Impoundments

You don't have to go too far back in bass-fishing history to find that "fishing the weeds" was the domain of the natural-lake angler. In the glacial lake belt from New England across the northern

This impoundment offers potential bass habitat between the bank and the channel. The stump and driftwood in the foreground indicate that there is good cover in the impoundment for bass.

third of the country almost to the edge of the Rockies, and in shallow, natural lakes of Florida, cover meant weedbeds. Weedbed edges were the important pivot points in bass movements. South of the Mason Dixon Line and north of the Florida border, however, where most bass fishing takes place in impoundments, timber has reigned as the supreme bass-holding cover, and the channel edge drop-off was the primary pivot point in bass movements.

How times change! Those weedbeds remain as important as ever in natural lakes, but vegetation is steadily becoming more and more of a factor in impoundments across the country. The impoundment-building boom is over. Without newly formed impoundments to fish, anglers need to learn the ways of bass in more mature environments.

As the non-aquatic forms of cover decay, the nutrient-rich en-

Impoundment bass fisheries are enjoying a rebirth in some areas because of the introduction of milfoil and hydrilla to these impoundments. This has reversed the usual birth-growth-decline cycle of many impoundments.

Impoundments

vironment, further fueled by the decay of the brush and timber, features rapid growth of aquatic plant life. While many impoundments follow the predictable growth and decline timetable, some of the impoundments, particularly in the South, built between the late '50s and early '70s have enjoyed a rebirth in recent years as milfoil and hydrilla which provide bass habitat have become established. The "good old days" returned to the Southern and mid-America impoundments belt—by some accounts, stronger than ever.

Unfortunately, the fertile habitat of many of those impoundments, combined with the types of vegetation that have been introduced to them, have created a whole new world of problems. For every bass angler who appreciates the beauty and desirability of a dense, surface-matted bed of milfoil, there is an average lake user, such as a sailor or water-skier, who cries foul over the presence of this "nasty seaweed" that ruins his sport. Impoundment anglers are now joining the battles over aquatic vegetation that natural-lake fishermen have been waging for years in some areas of the country.

Mistakes have been made on both fronts. The decline—virtual halt, really—in the bass fishery in Florida's Harris Chain of Lakes has been blamed by critics on ill-advised, chemical weed-control measures. Similar but not quite as severe misfortune has befallen once renown fisheries in Guntersville, Alabama, and Conroe, Texas. Vegetation is the key to continued health for many of the country's major impoundments. Learning the ways of bass in the weeds is a major step in staying in touch with those fish as the impoundments continue through their life cycles.

The Creek Channel

Even though the amounts of submerged vegetation in many impoundments is increasing, the fact remains that these impoundments were built by damming a river and its flood plain. The flooded creek channels remain the primary structural feature and continue to maintain their importance in the lives of bass. Feeder or side-creek channels provide the classic "highways" to the shallow, back ends of coves during the spring and fall. Ridges along the main channel edge, adjacent to the channel's intersection with side channels, are among the places in a reservoir most consistently used by bass. If weedbeds grow on these ridges now, so much the better. Anglers who find this situation definitely will be in "hawg" heaven.

The impoundment's structural configuration is still what guides fish movements. But the presence of vegetation undeniably affects fishing in a positive manner.

Riverine Sections

If you head far enough up a creek channel in an impoundment, whether it is a sizeable tributary or the main river channel, you eventually come to an area that functions more as a river than as an impoundment, where current is the primary factor in the lives of the fish. Where a stump, log or boulder is used as a current break rather than protective cover, the fish feed in the manner of river fish, letting the current wash food to them rather than hunting for it.

These areas can be extremely important during specific seasons. When the fall turnover has upset normal patterns of life in the main lake, these riverine areas continue to function normally and produce good catches.

12

Rivers And Streams

From wadable smallmouth streams to giant waterways that serve as industrial shipping lanes, rivers hold bass. Today, some of the best bass fishing in the country is available in flowing water. Our major rivers have been the beneficiaries of massive cleanup campaigns. Rivers like the Hudson, Susquehanna, Mississippi, Arkansas—once little more than shipping lanes and dumping grounds for waste products—are now teeming with gamefish. The water is cleaner and, in many cases, vegetation has either made a comeback or emerged for the first time as a viable environmental presence. Bass have found new territory to colonize.

River fishing can be much different than lake fishing. More fish spend more time relating to river shorelines and shallow-water areas. The factor determining where these fish will position themselves is the current. The ability to "read" the water— visualizing where the current flows strongest, where it flows the least, and where it creates an eddy or pocket of slack water—is the secret of the consistently successful NAFC river angler.

Life for a fish in a steady current requires expending considerably more energy than life in still waters. Thus, river bass feed more often and more aggressively than their lake-bred relatives. They go "off feed" less frequently, too. In essence, rivers can be looked upon by the bass angler as a quick solution to a difficult fishing situation. When a series of back-to-back weather systems puts bass activity on hold in your favorite lake, shifting your at-

Bass in rivers spend more time actively feeding in shallow water than bass that inhabit the still waters of lakes. River bass also are less likely to be adversely affected by the passage of fronts.

Rivers And Streams

tention to the nearest river can put you in contact with active, easily caught bass in very short order.

Free-Flowing Rivers

Most large rivers in the country flow unhindered by dams only in their tidal reaches. Therefore, free-flowing, non-tidal rivers generally are small, shallow and moderately fast. Whether they are best fished from a float boat or by wading, many of these rivers offer superb angling opportunities for smallmouth bass. From the Housatonic in Connecticut, to the New River in West Virginia and the Columbia River of the Pacific Northwest, anglers are re-learning the joy of fishing for scrappy fish in flowing water.

Smallmouths adapt best to river stretches that have few areas less than 3 feet deep and have "moderately flowing" waters. A gradient or stream-bed drop of 10 to 15 feet per mile is ideal, although smallmouths do thrive in a few small rivers which have somewhat faster flow.

River smallmouths are like fish that live in the current anywhere: They find feeding lies that offer them a view of the onrushing current without having to actually work or fight the current to maintain position. As could be expected, this equates to an affinity for current-obstructing boulders and deadfalls, and to current-deflecting structure like gravel bars. They spend more time in deep pools than in fast riffles and will often tuck into overhanging or undercut banks.

The diet of a river smallmouth is not unlike that of a large trout. Most of its insect consumption comes in the form of nymphs, and it relies heavily on crayfish and assorted stream resident baitfish, like sculpins, chubs and dace. Being the ever-opportunistic predator that it is, the river-bred smallie will also relate to windfall feeding situations that force non-native life-forms (terrestrials) into the stream or take a shot at whatever potential meal happens to wash downstream. The current in a river acts as a conveyor belt for food, and in these small, fairly fast streams, that belted conveyor of food is moving quickly, so the resident smallies must react to a potential meal quickly. If it doesn't turn out to be food, they can always expel it. Unless, of course, it has a hook in it.

Small-river smallmouths are rather small in size—10 to 13 inches for the most part, but 3- to 4-pound fish are possible in most

Look for hotspots wherever the river's current breaks, forming eddies. Flecks of foam on the water's surface are a tip-off of what's happening below the surface. Cast to the foam.

any stream that holds smallies. Larger rivers—typically, those fished more comfortably from a boat than by wading—can produce much larger specimens.

Wadable streams should fit into the fishing activities of even the most serious, impoundment- or lake-based bass angler. They offer a great fishing opportunity under cold-front conditions that may turn still-water bass completely off. In this situation, it is much easier to study the way fish position themselves in current and to learn to "read" a river. That knowledge, once gained in the "classroom" of a small- to medium-sized, wadable stream, can easily be applied to larger rivers and to the riverine sections of impoundments. Of course, fishing these rivers is rewarding in its own right, as well.

Dammed Rivers

Most of the larger rivers in the country are a series of dammed pools. Some of these pools, but certainly not all, function more as impoundments than as rivers. If the dam inundates portions of a river's flood plain (other than seasonally) or creates more areas of slack water than flowing water, it might be classified better as an impoundment or flowage than as a river.

In some of the larger rivers, the largemouth bass is an incidental occurrence in the main river area where smallmouth or spotted bass dominate. The largemouths, though, usually own the backwaters and possibly certain reduced-current areas in the main river. In heavily current-influenced areas, features like wing dams, natural points and bridge abutments divert the current, creating large eddies and, just as importantly, backwashes or reduced current areas that can act as mini-environments. These are seasonal home areas for largemouths. Of course, to hold bass, it's necessary for these areas to offer more than just limited current flow. Obviously, abundant feeding opportunities are foremost among the necessary elements.

Spotted bass often school heavily in larger rivers, and relate almost exclusively to steep, bluff-type shorelines and to steep, rip-rap banks that break directly into the river channel. Smallmouths, on the other hand, prefer sand or gravel bars, or areas where the river flows over deep boulders. Largemouths in the main river invariably will be scattered, and related almost solely to individual current breaks like fallen trees and the pilings along seawalls.

In most dammed rivers that are still used as shipping lanes, locks provide a unique feeding opportunity. Especially where smallmouths are present, these locks may well be a key element in productive fishing patterns. Fishing around the outflow gates of the locks as the water is being released can put you onto large numbers of very aggressive bass.

When heavy rains create muddy conditions, rivers are affected first. Fast-flowing, muddy water can make fishing difficult—especially in the fall and winter when falling water temperatures may have bass going into a reduced state of activity. By themselves, cold, muddy and swiftly flowing waters present challenges. Combine the three, though, and you are face-to-face with bass fishing's biggest challenge. The solution? Usually it means finding water that is insulated or isolated from at least one of the three negative factors.

That might mean locking through a few dams, either upstream or down, to get away from the muddiest water. Or it could mean concentrating on a warm-water discharge below a power plant in order to eliminate the cold part of the fishing equation.

Small rivers can be dammed to raise the water level in certain areas. These small dams create pools, resulting in great bass hotspots under the right conditions.

Or it could mean moving into a backwater area where the mud and cold exist, but the swift flow doesn't. And finally, if the river supports any vegetation, it may mean fishing as far back in the weeds as possible, where the vegetation's current-buffering capability and its ability to filter the particulate matter that's mucking up the water are most pronounced.

Tidal Rivers

The tidally influenced environment is one of the unique and interesting places to study bass behavior. For one thing, you get many opportunities to work with very active bass. The tidal environment doesn't allow much time for bass to become inactive because they must adjust almost constantly to the changing conditions. The water level rises and recedes twice a day, and, in most

Catching bass in tidal areas presents a whole new set of challenges for the serious bass fisherman. The good news is that the higher energy needs for these bass requires them to eat more often.

instances, the current flow actually reverses direction, disrupting and moving the slack-water pockets where bass might otherwise be inclined to rest.

The highly energy-consumptive life of a bass in a tidal-water situation means that it must eat more often than a bass in a "normal" situation. That means the angler must stay in contact with forage that may be moving considerable distances with the changing tides. It also means that individual bass may adopt several different feeding styles for the different conditions they face daily.

The most commonly recognized tidewater bass-feeding strategy involves the bass taking advantage of the displaced forage being washed out of expansive, shallow flats and marshes with the receding tide. Positioning near outlet creeks and ditches forming tidal marshes, bass can capitalize on this abundant forage. You could call it a windfall feeding opportunity; however, because it happens twice a day, it's really more a matter of "business as usual" for the bass.

The feeding activity involving the last half of a falling tide is so great a factor that in most tidal rivers the best catches are invariably made in summer and early fall by anglers who key on it exclusively. The tidal cycles run later the farther up the river you go, so it's possible with modern, high-performance boats to make contact with the feeding binge several times in several different locations during each cycle. Depending upon the width, depth and contour of the riverbed, low tide can arrive as much as an hour later just 15 miles farther up the river.

Experienced tidewater anglers time their trips to coincide with the last half of the falling tide at the downstream end of the river, following that part of the cycle upriver.

While the end of the falling tide concentrates aggressively feeding bass into easy-to-identify, confined areas, it is not the only option. On an incoming tide, some bass instinctively move to areas of reduced current—perhaps to conserve some energy before the next tidally influenced feeding period. Others, though, follow their prey back into the shallow cover, often into areas that were dry only a few hours earlier.

Capitalizing on this type of behavior calls for a completely different approach. Rather than holding at current breaks and picking off food being washed downstream, the bass are scattering back into the cover-heavy, shallow flats, chasing after bait. Covering as much water as possible with spinnerbaits, buzzbaits or weedless spoons works best in this situation.

13

Ponds

P rior to the building of impoundments across the country and the environmental cleanup campaign of the past few decades to reclaim our rivers, bass fishing was considered a small-water pastime in many areas of the country. Developments over the past 25 years have diverted most bass fishing interest toward the larger waters, but bass still swim and still offer exceptional fishing opportunities in ponds and other downsized environments.

Technically, a pond is an artificial impoundment shallow enough to support rooted vegetation across its entire expanse. In the real fishing world, however, almost any small body of still or nearly still water is viewed as a pond.

Even to the angler whose primary interest is in tournament fishing or learning a big body of water, small ponds represent an ideal classroom in which to develop theories which can then be applied to larger waters. Bass living in small natural lakes, farm ponds, stock tanks, strip pits, gravel pits and oxbow lakes (cut off from rivers by years of erosion and sedimentation) have the same basic instincts as their relatives in larger waters. Of course, generations of genetic straining have tuned their instincts to maximize adaptation to the less diverse environments in which they live, but their natural function still is as a predator.

For that reason, ponds offer exceptional learning opportunities to study how bass respond to weather changes and various stimuli in specific situations. A bass angler who doesn't spend

A major advantage of pond fishing is that NAFC Members don't need a boat to enjoy the fruits of bass fishing. As indicated here, good-sized bass are only a cast away.

time getting intimately familiar with these pond residents is missing out on a golden educational opportunity. And, on a lot of fishing enjoyment.

Because heading off across the lake in search of a more productive area is not a viable option here, fishing a miniature body of water allows—or forces—you to concentrate more on things like analyzing how fish respond to various presentations, how they position themselves in relation to specific structural configurations or cover under various weather conditions, how to identify what conditions give them lockjaw and how to best overcome bad conditions.

Of course, pond fishing can be far more than just a learning experience for larger bodies of water, as well. The opportunity to fish without the distractions common to bigger waters—skiers, commercial traffic and lots of other fishermen—is an attractive alternative. (So is the opportunity to possibly catch a huge fish!) Because smaller bodies of water are simpler environments and offer the bass fewer options, it is easier to locate and catch big fish on small waters. And make no mistake about it—small waters do grow big bass.

The excellent fishing they provide, along with other advantages, makes ponds and smaller waters the preferred fisheries for many bass anglers. It's advisable to find a selection of small waters close to home that offers a variety of habitat options—perhaps a dug farm pond or two, a small natural lake, an oxbow or small river. Cumulatively, a selection of such confined environments, although each may be fairly simple on its own, offers a choice of varied fishing situations and a chance to "rotate the crops" so-to-speak, rather than constantly hammering away at one limited population of bass.

Pond fishing is unique in two ways: The simpler environment offers fewer habitat options so the bulk of the pond's bass population is usually doing the same thing at the same time, and attention to detail is paramount for anglers. A "point" that extends a few yards from the shoreline and drops off from a 3-foot-deep flat into an 8-foot-deep basin might warrant a cast or two by an angler fishing a large body of water. In a pond, a feature fitting that description can be a major structural element where most of the bass in the pond feed at one time or another!

When fishing miniaturized waters, many anglers automati-

Working a pond with a boat is still convenient, especially on the larger ponds or those with cover spread throughout. Taking bass in their home environment is especially exciting.

Anglers should resist the temptation to "downsize" presentations because they are fishing a pond. Pond bass are opportunistic and often respond to outsized lures. Downsizing often is counter-productive with plastic worms, jigs and surface plugs.

cally scale down their presentation as well. This is appropriate with "high-impact" presentations—those that involve a lot of flash or vibration—because after not too many casts, every active bass in a small pond may have been exposed to the presentation. It's less advantageous, and possibly even counter-productive, with plastic worms, jigs, surface plugs and the like. Pond bass tend to be even more opportunistic than their large-lake relatives, and often respond readily to outsized lures.

Pond-fishing strategies are determined in accordance with the less varied habitat options that ponds provide. From a standpoint of cover, ponds tend toward one of two extremes—either almost devoid of it (like strip pits and some golf-course ponds) or overrun with brush, stumps or vegetation. In the first instance, you'd most likely leave the flipping stick home. In the second, you might not take anything else!

Presentation choices, too, are limited by the nature of the pond because the dominant condition is likely to exist throughout a small body of water. If, like in so many small ponds, the bottom is covered with a layer of slimy algae, deep-diving plugs and heavy jigs function more like dredges than fishing lures. If a deep diver is covered with goo three cranks into the retrieve or a jig buries itself in the bottom moss as soon as it sinks; these presentations become a waste of time. If the condition exists pretty much throughout the pond, you're limited to floating plugs, weightless plastic worms and spinnerbaits.

The smallest ponds are usually best fished from shore. It's important to keep in mind that in the limited environment of a pond, the shoreline's breakline is just as important as it is in waters you would fish from a boat. More fish usually can be caught in small ponds by casting roughly parallel to the shoreline than by casting out toward the middle of the pond. Working around the perimeter of the pond, you should cast ahead of your path to learn about the conditions in that pond—where the shoreline is steep (Steep shoreline in some ponds drops off into 3 feet of water 4 feet from the bank.) and where there is an extended shallow lip.

You'll soon discover that even in the smallest ponds, bass frequent certain areas of the shoreline, and avoid certain areas or use them only incidentally. With the importance placed on small structure because of the pond's size, a small point, a bank cut a few feet wide, a couple small rocks or an exposed root along an otherwise clean bank can be important. Work each potential bass-holding spot thoroughly.

14

Competition And Coexistence

ass don't live in a vacuum. While they adapt well enough to use areas that are much less than prime habitat, bass face competition in many lakes from species which are more ideally suited to some portions of that habitat. When that happens, they become secondary, or part-time, users of that habitat or do not partake of that particular habitat and feeding option at all.

As striped bass and hybrid stripers are introduced into more and more impoundments across the country, they take over the more open sections of the environment. Striper proponents claim that there is little or no competition between the two species. To a certain extent, that's true. Stripers and hybrids are more suited to life in open water and actually compete more directly with their cousin, the white bass. However, at least one study has indicated that the introduction of any one of those species has detrimental effects on the black-bass population.

All three species in question are basically open-water predators, and compete directly with each other, primarily for shad. Because the white bass are already present in most impoundments, impact on black bass from the introduction of stripers and hybrids is negligible. Black bass do relate heavily to the shad, though, and there is little doubt that a presence from the striper, hybrid or white bass species in an environment occupied by bass has some effect on the bass population. It simply limits or curtails their ability to use one potential prey/habitat option.

Showing how adaptable these fish can be, shallow-water bass will often adopt the lifestyle of a walleye or striper to take advantage of an offshore forage base, as if filling an ecological vacuum.

Competition And Coexistence

Stripers—or pike, for that matter—may force black bass to avoid certain areas of a lake. This obviously reduces the number of habitat options for bass; the angler needs to be aware of this.

An environmental niche that could have supported a number of black bass is taken up by these fish. Whether or not it is good for the fishery is not the point. These are impoundments, after all, and none of the fish in question is native to them, because there's no such thing as being native to an artificial environment.

In natural lakes, offshore largemouth populations are far less common where walleye are present, and northern pike have a direct effect on offshore smallmouth populations. All of these fish compete for the same food source, and often share the same territories.

In a "pure" bass lake, where the largemouth is the only predator in its position in the food chain, all of the potential feeding grounds are available to it. Semi-independent bass populations often develop, and each lives differently because of the different habitat options available in the lake. (Habitat options, in this case, are built around food sources).

The more individual, isolated spawning areas existing in any given lake, the more likely independent bass populations will develop. If spawning grounds are extensive and not isolated from each other, the potential effects of the genetic straining factor on specific population groups are minimized by interbreeding among these groups.

In many lakes, independent population groups almost never interact with each other through the spring and summer; yet they may winter together in what fisheries biologists call a *seasonal aggregation*. Finding these winter aggregations can be the key to determining what a lake truly has to offer in terms of bass-fishing potential.

It's not uncommon for a lake to be considered "runt city" all season long, for instance, yet produce good-sized bass late in the fall. Those bigger fish do not suddenly materialize in cold water, and their existence proves that there are separate population groups relating to habitat options undiscovered or unexplored by the majority of the fishermen who frequent the lake. The opportunity to investigate a situation like this is something no avid and inquisitive bass angler can afford to pass up.

═══════15═══════

Environmental Stability

Serious anglers are constantly looking for indications of what bass might be doing at any given time. Many have started to measure environmental factors that they suspect influence the whereabouts and activity of bass.

Wouldn't it be wonderful if a chart could be devised that would predict exactly what bass might be doing in, say, 58-degree F water or in water with a pH of 7.4 or with 6ppm dissolved oxygen content? Manufacturers of equipment designed to measure those variables might like anglers to believe that they actually can. Anglers who have experimented with these things have noted, though, it just isn't that simple.

Everything is relative. And combinations of the variables do not necessarily add up in a perfectly linear fashion. Perhaps if all bass lived in the same environment, they would react in the same way to a change in conditions. But environments vary, and the reactions of bass to seemingly similar condition changes differ greatly from one environment to the next.

Their incredible flexibility/adaptability allows bass to function effectively in such a wide range of environmental conditions that specific water temperature/water chemistry values are almost meaningless. Temperature and water chemistry must be within the fish's survival range. And the survival range for a bass is wide. For instance, a pH level that might send bass looking for more hospitable conditions in one environment might be as close to optimum as they ever experience in another.

Bass often retreat to places that are the least influenced by external forces, especially when the fall cooling trend takes place. This catch was taken just off of a steep bluff bank.

Environmental Stability

More important than the specific values of each of the notable variables (within the fish's survival range) are changes in those values. Sudden and drastic changes in water temperature and/or chemistry appear to have a decidedly detrimental effect on bass activity. It may be that the severity of the change is more the culprit than the actual value of the variable. Environmental stability is the key to sustained bass action. Stable conditions result in predictable bass activity. Slowly improving conditions forecast increased activity; slowly deteriorating conditions may or may not diminish bass activity. With a few notable exceptions, rapid changes in any conditions, even those that seem like they should promote imcreased bass activity, are usually followed by a period of slow fishing as the bass adjust to the changes. The lower their metabolic rate, the longer it takes them to adjust to the conditions.

An important consideration is how seasonally appropriate the change is. In spring, warming trends are good; cooling trends are bad. In summer, warming trends and stable conditions are good, slow cooling trends have almost no effect, and severe cold fronts are bad. In fall and early winter, it mostly depends upon the depth that the bass are located. For taking shallow bass, slow cooling trends are good; warming trends are bad in the short-term but if they last at least a few days, they can result in good fishing. If the fish have already set up in wintering areas, where external changes have little impact, current weather conditions have virtually no effect upon fishing success.

Areas that are insulated from changes in conditions offer more predictable activity. It might not be the best fishing available in any given situation, but it is almost invariably the steadiest. For the most part, this means that deep-water patterns are less likely to fall apart overnight than patterns based on fish activity in shallow water. Likewise, "main lake patterns" are more resistant to change than those based in isolated bays or other confined areas. The volume of water in main lake sections is an effective buffer, causing changes that result from weather conditions to be more gradual and less intense.

Remember that the zone of awareness of a bass is limited. It doesn't know that there's more food available on the next point across the way or that water temperatures are more favorable somewhere else. When conditions turn for the worse, a bass usually will decrease its activity level—even to the point of going

In cold water, bass assume a non-aggressive attitude in response to a sudden change in conditions; it lasts longer because their metabolic rate is slowed. An angler has to be more patient, and adjust his presentations.

semi-dormant—and ride out the discomfort. If conditions change too drastically or too rapidly for this to be a safe option, bass may be forced to vacate an area. The key is that they are being driven away from something, not necessarily attracted to something else.

Seasonal Considerations

Environmental stability is an extremely important factor during the coldest part of winter. With their metabolism slowed by the low water temperature, bass take a long time to recover from sudden changes in conditions. In some cases, the length of time can be physically stressful to the bass.

In latitudes where the cold-water season is quite long, bass that are repelled by condition fluctuations at times when they can't effectively deal with them move to areas where those fluctuations are the least severe. In rivers, that usually means someplace outside the current—a slow-moving side creek or dredged-out marina basin, for instance. In any environment where it's available, a hard-bottomed (non-organic) area in water deep enough to absorb sudden changes in water temperature or content before reaching the bass will be piled thick with fish by the time the water temperature passes through the 40s.

If the only deep water available is stagnant and occurs in con-

As weather conditions slowly improve, so does the bass activity. Some of the best fishing may occur during this recovery period—it pays to be on the water during this time.

junction with an organic, mucky bottom, the fish will most likely suspend. They may suspend in submerged treetops if that's an option of that particular environment, or they may simply hold in open water some distance off the bottom. They remain relatively inactive during this period, but are not necessarily dormant.

Frequently Fluctuating Environments

Perhaps one of the most difficult aspects of environmental stability to grasp is that predictable change is a form of stability. This is most often observed with current flow and water level in many impoundments and even more so in tidal rivers. If fluctuations occur on a frequent and regular basis, they become the normal routine for the residents of that environment. An interruption in that normal routine amounts to a change in conditions.

Impoundments offer bass anglers some unique challenges. Fluctuating water levels affect fish activity cycles because current flow from power generation seems to trigger a feeding mode.

Environmental Stability

In many power-generation impoundments, the daily opening of the generators and the resultant increase in current flow triggers fish to launch into a feeding mode. When the generators are shut down for a few days for maintenance, the normal cycles of fish activity are disrupted. It may take a week or more after the normal cycle begins anew for the fish to adjust completely.

The Worst Common Denominator

It's been established that bass are adaptable. They seem to find some way to survive in environments that are pretty far outside the bounds of what might be considered optimum conditions for bass. In bodies of water where the vast majority of the available area is only marginally suited to bass, the bass find the area or areas that come closest to their needs.

Find a pocket of marginally less threatening conditions, and you've most likely found a bass hotspot. Whether all, or even most, of the bass have found such a spot is a moot point because those that have set up camp in an area that's even a bit friendlier are going to be easier to catch, and they're going to stay put unless the conditions that forced them there change. If you know where there are a number of bass, it's better to invest time learning how to catch them than wasting it searching for scattered and possibly inactive fish.

In a harsh environment, the factor that is farthest outside of a bass' environmental needs or changes the most drastically can often be the key to bass location. Avoiding life threatening or physically stressful conditions is among the strongest instincts attributed to a bass.

It is your job as a bass angler to compare the places in which more than a stray bass or two are frequently found in any given body of water. This should be an effort to find the common link that makes all those possibly diverse spots somehow more suitable for the bass than other places in the lake—a search for the common denominator, so to speak.

Other than food, bass are most concerned about avoiding unsuitable conditions. The common denominator you are looking for is the "worst common denominator." What negative condition in a specific environment are bass the most likely to avoid at all costs?

The resident bass in a lake that is generally marginal in pH, for instance, could well be very sensitive to seemingly minor fluctuations in the acid/alkaline balance of the water. Or, the bass in waters with frequent and drastic changes in temperature would most likely find conditions less stressful in areas that didn't undergo those changes or where the changes were buffered by some other aspect of the environment.

Identifying the factor that bass in any given environment find most necessary to avoid can go a long way toward helping find additional habitats that they are likely to use. It can be a tedious and frustrating process. Often, you're operating on theory alone, and then investing hours, days or even months of fishing time in proving or disproving the theory. The best thing about fishing on theory is that it provides a driving reason to fish more (under different conditions) in an attempt to promote it from theory to guideline or demote it to bunk. To an avid bass angler, anything that justifies more time spent fishing is a benefit!

Presentation

=16=

Activity Levels

T here are anglers who are quick to assign variations in bass activity to solunar influence while others see "solunar tables" as laughable superstition. Most seem intrigued by the concept but are unwilling to put their full faith in it. Simple observation indicates that various forms of wildlife are more active at certain times than at others. That activity in nature seems to follow some sort of repetitive cycle with a certain degree of unison, or more accurately, intertwined active/ inactive periods, among various species. It also appears that the farther down the food chain, the stronger these influences— whatever their cause—are.

As the most developed species—the only species with true reasoning power and intellect—humans are much too far removed from such primeval forces to consciously recognize them. That's not to say that mankind isn't influenced in some manner, but it's not an overriding power, at least at a conscious level.

Even though the argument that such forces exist is strong, the argument in favor of any of the published tables being accurate is much less convincing. Anyone who has kept accurate and unbiased records of catch rates and compared them to the popular charts of predicted gamefish activity can only believe the accuracy and dependability of those charts by choosing to ignore the large numbers of fish, including lunker fish, caught during the "off peak" times, and the "peak" times that pass with not even a nibble or a nudge.

It's not impossible to catch moderately inactive bass. They can be taken by using a slow-moving presentation. The trick is to keep the lure in front of their noses for as long as possible.

Activity Levels

Accept that unseen or unperceived forces influence fish activity to some degree. But temper that acceptance with the knowledge that other, more recognizable stimuli also enter into the mix. Some, like the beginning and end of the photoperiod (daylight) occur on a regular schedule and are thus predictable. Local weather conditions—the daily weather and general trends in the weather—are not as predictable. This can be proved by comparing the U.S. Weather Service's long-range projections with actual weather. Or, for that matter, compare last night's television weather forecast with the actual weather today.

Anglers should also understand that activity level and catchability are not necessarily interchangeable concepts. Bass activity in some situations might well be triggered by the general inactivity (and corresponding ease of capture) of particular prey species. Some researchers have noted yellow perch as being among the species that display activity patterns most accurately attributed to lunar influence tables. Is it more than coincidental that muskellunge and walleye (the predators that feed most heavily on yellow perch) are the ones that catch records indicate are actually contrary to the so-called solunar charts? Is it not possible—even likely—that similar relationships exist between lower life-forms made inactive by an ebb in lunar influence and the opportunistic bass?

Because the bass is a predator whose chief activity involves feeding, the "catchability" of a bass at any given time is proportionally related to its activity level. There are exceptions, of course. During the few hours that bass are actually engaged in spawning, they are in a high state of activity; however, they may be virtually impossible to catch. This is because their activity and attention is directed toward something other than feeding or protecting territory. A few hours later, when they are no longer so obviously active, they might be easier to catch. It's not a matter of them going on feed, but simply of not being so singlemindedly active. They are easier to distract.

Still, the primary activity for a bass for much of the year involves feeding. Therefore, the higher its level of activity, the more likely it is to feed—or to make a feeding related response to a lure.

To better understand bass activity levels, think in terms of windows or zones. Everyone has heard of a fish's "strike zone." But

An angler can vary presentations considerably when dealing with aggressive fish because these bass will chase anything that even remotely looks like food to them.

because the bass has such a limited world, a serious angler needs to be even more aware of the space immediately surrounding the fish. Call it the bass' "zone of awareness." It's exactly what it sounds like: the area in which a bass is aware of your lure, or anything else for that matter. In addition to the awareness zone and the strike zone, imagine another defined zone: the reaction or response zone. It's almost the same as the strike zone, but takes into account that the reaction of a bass to a lure or bait isn't always a strike! Sometimes, it seems that it's more often alarm or intimidation!

Actually, there are distinct "zones of awareness" for each of a fish's senses, and they each change size and shape depending upon various factors. Both the "strike zone" and the "reaction zone" expand and contract in relation to the bass' relative activity level; however, they can never extend beyond the zone of awareness. A bass cannot react to something it is not aware of. That applies to your lure as well as to an injured minnow 20 feet away. It also applies to non-feeding situations. A bass in 30 feet of water—beyond the level of light penetration and certainly far beyond the reach of short-term warming trends, isn't going to react to a warm, sunny day by coming up into the shallows to feed. It doesn't know what's going on there, and can't react to it.

The reaction zone of a bass can, however, be much smaller

than its awareness zone, depending upon its state of activity. The awareness zones are influenced primarily by external conditions. The most obvious is that water clarity affects the size of the bass' visual awareness zone. Current certainly plays a role in the shape and extent of the visual, audible and chemo-receptive awareness zones, all of which extend much farther upstream than down.

Divers have noted that when a bass is particularly logy, it almost seems that its zone of awareness shrinks to almost nothing. Everyone has seen bass in shallow water that simply refuse to react to anything. As opposed to being spooky, bass in this condition seem almost to be in suspended animation. For all intents and purposes, they might as well not have a zone of awareness. It's open to question as to whether something causes them to actually shut down their senses or if it's just a matter of their reaction zone receding to basically nothing. Then again, it doesn't matter if a bass doesn't notice your lure bumping into its nose or notices but ignores it; you're not going to catch that bass.

The reason for discussing totally dormant bass is to make clear just how inactive they can be. Some observers feel that this "suspended animation" mode is a defense mechanism which allows bass to ride out the more difficult conditions. It is sort of like short-term hibernation. Even though there is no scientific proof to back this theory, it does offer plausible explanation for the bass' occasional total lockjaw.

Aggressive

Aggressive bass: The bass anglers love to find! They are on feed and will not hesitate to strike from long range. Aggressive fish are those whose strike zones reach the limits of their awareness zones. It doesn't take much to convince these bass that something might be worth some exertion.

Non-feeding bass also can be aggressive—especially during the spawning season when they may be protecting their territory or their nests.

Active

These bass are a step below aggressive. These are feeding fish; however, their strike zones do not necessarily reach the limits of their awareness zones. Still, certain triggers can effectively extend their strike zone by causing them to move toward something that

Dark skies signaling an impending front indicates that bass will most likely be aggressive. This results in fun on the water.

interests them. They may chase after a lure, but they don't necessarily commit to striking it until they get within range. They may be waiting until they have the object within their narrow zone of binocular vision which not only improves their visual perception of the lure, but makes striking an effort with a greater chance of success.

This theory also accounts for the all-too-frequent case of a bass following and closing in on a lure, then flaring off to the side at almost the last possible moment. While it's been suggested that bass do this when they see the boat or the angler, keep in mind that bass really don't know what a boat is. Those that have been caught previously may associate it with a stressful occurrence and turn off. It's just as likely, however, that when the bass gets the lure into its area of binocular vision, and suddenly sees it in 3-D, it

Activity Levels

Whether bass are in a negative mode or just neutral, it pays to quickly check known bass hangouts, such as this reed line, occasionally to see if the fish have become active again.

notices some aspect of the lure that alarms it or simply identifies the lure as being something other than food.

Neutral

Probably the most common activity state is neutral. Throughout much of the year, more bass are neutral more of the time than active, aggressive, negative or dormant. Neutral bass are less inclined to move very far or very fast to investigate a possible meal, and almost never make a strike commitment until or unless they are in fairly close to a potential meal. However, they are definitely catchable.

Negative

Negative-mode bass are not quite dormant. They are not prone to strike, but can be caught—usually by using a painstakingly slow approach. The visual aspect of their awareness zone may be reduced substantially because they do not necessarily lie in "feeding position" with a view of open water; they may have their heads buried in cover. Still, their reaction zone—at least the negative aspect of it—can be large. These fish are skittish or spooky.

Complete Angler's Library

Dormant

Dormant bass were discussed earlier in this chapter. If they're in shallow water, and you can find them easily, check on them once in a while. They won't stay dormant forever.

Defining activity states by neatly pigeonholing them into identifiable categories makes them easier to understand; however, like everything else, activity states come in degrees. The definitions used here only describe the primary colors, so-to-speak. Just as there are myriad shades of green—from aqua to chartreuse—between blue and yellow, there are limitless variations in a bass' state of activity ranging between active and neutral or aggressive and active.

Individual bass may exhibit slightly to extremely varied responses to the same conditions. Identifying a few bass as being in one general range of the activity scale will help in developing a pattern that will work on a lot of bass that are most likely within few a degrees either way of that range.

=17=

Location Versus Position

B ass fishing's world is full of sayings that fall somewhere between axiom and cliche. Many of them deal with the importance of locating bass. While these sayings may seem overly simplistic, they all contain kernels of truth that are worth considering by serious bass fishermen. Such as:

You've got to find 'em before you can catch 'em.

Catching bass is a matter of 90 percent location and 10 percent presentation.

You can't catch 'em where they ain't.

Catching bass is like selling real estate—location, location, location.

The cliche, "You can't catch 'em where they ain't," should make it obvious that location is paramount. But if you fail to recognize that position and location are not quite the same thing, and don't take into account the relationship between the bass' position and its activity level, you may have trouble catching them where they are!

Location is where, within the lake, bass are. Narrowing down their location is the first, and arguably the most important, step in catching them. In traditional bass fishing philosophy, presentation is the next logical step. But within any given location, there are numerous potential positions bass might hold, depending upon the layout of the breaks and cover, and on their particular state of activity.

In the advanced bass fisherman's philosophy, presentation decisions are a factor of the position the fish are in or the position to

Flipping the shoreline cover often results in a challenge from some really big bass. If you ease in quietly onto the cover, they won't be able to resist bait coming down through a pocket.

Location Versus Position   171

be probed for fish. Position is exactly how the fish are situated in relation to whatever structural elements exist in their location. A weedbed or point is location. A corner along the edge of that weedbed or a stump on the point is location refined to a very narrow degree. Exactly where a bass is in relation to that corner or stump, (near, over, under, shaded side, sunny side) and which direction it's facing, as well, constitutes position.

While location is a factor of the habitat (the forage base and the existing weather and water conditions) position is primarily a factor of the bass' activity state. Position, of course, can be affected by weather and water conditions, but is much more complex. Being so directly related to the bass' activity state, position should be a determining factor in the choice of presentation.

In practical, on-the-water application, position and presentation become inexorably linked. The bass' position provides clues as to what type of presentation might be best suited to catching them. The types of presentations that get a response from bass help us refine our judgment of their position and activity state, thereby aiding in making "adjustments" in fishing methods and casting target selection.

The bass' role as a predator demands that the active bass be positioned to strike. In dense cover, active bass are likely to be in ambush position, near the edge of the cover and close to the overhead canopy of that cover. There they gain maximum camouflage advantage because of the contrast between their position in the shade and the position of any prey passing by in the brightly lit areas. The predator can easily see out of the darkness, but prey exposed in the sunlight cannot see in. The effect is not unlike a car with deeply tinted windows.

It might help to think of the relationship between a bass' activity state and its position relative to cover as an analogy of pitching a baseball. The position just described, for an active but non-chasing bass, is high and inside. A bass that's low and inside— tucked into the most concave configuration of the cover— is almost invariably an inactive bass in the neutral to negative range. High and outside positioning usually indicates an aggressive bass. Low and outside is the most difficult to define. Bass in this position can be aggressive or passive. A lot depends upon the primary forage available to them. If it is crayfish, low and outside would be the natural position for aggressive fish. If the primary

Analyzing Parts Of Weedbeds

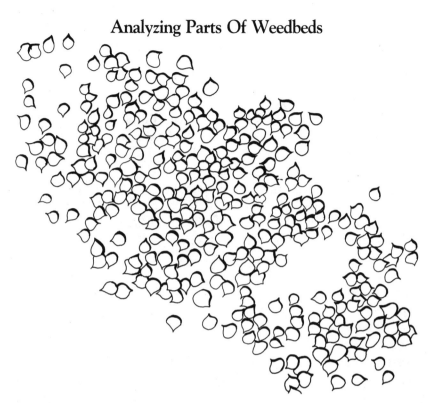

Cuts, turns and pockets in lily-pad beds or other visible weedbeds are clues to what's underneath. This hole (right) could be a stump, rock or depression in the bottom—all good reasons to fish it. These scattered pads (left) probably indicate a rather gradual change in the depth or bottom composition.

forage was open-water baitfish of one type or another, low and outside might indicate a neutral mood, or perhaps even dormancy!

Differences in the cover—especially certain types of wood cover—can further help identify the likely mood and activity level of bass using an area. Finely spaced cover—thick bushes, recently fallen trees and similar items—offer superb cover for small fish, but make maneuvering difficult for larger fish like bass. Bulkier cover, like stumps and old, dead fallen trees on which only the larger branches remain, can be great bass hideaways; however, they offer considerably less security for panfish.

When checking an area full of the first type of cover, it's wise to gear your approach to aggressive fish. Bass don't have "resting" conditions in such an area, and those that use it are typically hunting food as opposed to waiting to ambush food. They prowl the edges of the cover's thickest portions, looking for stray or otherwise accessible preyfish that have wandered away from the thick cover's security. Especially in clear-water situations, bass in this position are prone to make strike decisions as soon as a potential meal enters their awareness zone. If they didn't, their prey might easily escape into the cover before the bass could react.

Location And Position Affect Presentation

Finding and catching bass is a matter of locating them and figuring out what they are likely to bite on. Because the largemouth is so flexible, it has so many different food sources and can use so many different habitat options. Therefore, there are usually many potentially productive combinations of location/position/presentation under various combinations of weather and water conditions. If you had to try everything in your tackle box at every spot you thought might hold a fish, you'd never get anywhere.

Obviously, no one does that. Instead, anglers rely on their experience and their hunches to make educated guesses about what bass will likely respond to in certain situations. By tuning in to the relationship between a bass' activity level and its position, anglers can narrow the range of possibilities and make those guesses considerably more accurate. By applying knowledge of a lake's forage base to the formula, they further reduce the guesswork. One should know what a bass in a certain type of area is likely to eat at any given time of the year or time of the day within reasonable limits. It is that food, after all, that caused that bass to take up residence in that area in the first place.

Therefore, if fishing in areas that most likely hold bass because of the crayfish populations, use lures that simulate crayfish; use shad-imitating lures in areas that bass are likely to frequent only when they're on a heavy shad bite. The habitat being checked offers clues as to what types of prey might live there, and this is what any resident bass is likely to key on. Ignoring those clues does not constitute intelligent fishing.

Fish residing in and around heavy shoreline cover are most likely opportunistic feeders so lures should be chosen primarily for their ability to perform in the cover and to evoke responses from bass in specific positions. Be sure to fish the cover's outside edges, especially places where the cover configuration forms some type of protrusion. Presentations should be selected to appeal to actively feeding and aggressive bass. This means an up-tempo, horizontal approach.

Likewise, check the inside corners and crevices in that cover with presentations designed to draw a response from less-active bass. Slower, more vertically oriented presentations—like jigs or plastic worms—will work here. In particularly nasty looking spots (heavy cover where it's almost impossible to get a lure in, and twice as difficult to retrieve it) roll out the really subtle stuff, invest the time to get it into position and then let it stay there. Try to nudge it (without moving it) every now and then. Play the percentages by investing the most time and effort in the places that few anglers ever fish thoroughly.

18

Triggers And IDP

Triggers? IDP? What are these things? How do they fit into bass-catching strategies? You might call them cues or stimuli. However you refer to them, they are the specific aspects of a presentation to which bass actually respond. Things like color, shape, size, action and vibration, along with speed and proximity. All of these specific characteristics combine to form a presentation's identity profile (IDP).

Depending on a variety of factors but primarily on the fish's activity level, a specific cue might be a positive trigger, a negative trigger or a non-factor at any given moment in any given situation. The term non-factor is chosen for lure design elements that a bass might totally ignore, simply because "neutral trigger" seems rather oxymoronic. Some triggers that could be positive in the context of one identity profile could become negative cues or non-factors in a different IDP or under different conditions.

An accurate representation of some common prey can be a positive trigger, prompting a strike from a moderately active bass. That same lure, though, painted fluorescent orange (giving it an unnatural or intimidating appearance) might trigger that same fish to retreat farther into cover. Yet lures with a fluorescent color or loud, mechanical rattle—qualities that are totally foreign to natural prey—can be extremely effective, positive triggers when presented to more active bass.

Many lure design elements can work as two different things: an advertiser and a response generator. Advertisers help alert bass

In certain instances, bass can be coerced into attacking lures that are much larger than the size range of their normal prey. This often is true during the pre-spawn period when they're territorial and very aggressive.

Triggers And IDP

to the presence of a lure; response generators are what bass respond to once they are aware of the lure. When bass are very active, factors in the first category (advertisers) may be much more important than those in the second. In essence, the simple existence of a lure may be all the strike trigger a bass needs. The more you can reach out and grab that attention, the more strike responses you'll get from fish.

Conversely, when a fish's activity level is low, it doesn't take many negative cues to dissuade fish from responding to a lure as a potential meal. Presentation styles that are high in advertiser qualities are basically unnatural, and can be high in negative response when offered to the wrong bass at the wrong time. Most of the diet of a bass consists of creatures that are naturally camouflaged and don't do anything to unnecessarily alert the bass to their presence. Triggers or cues that fall outside the natural range should be avoided unless any positive aspects they bring to the advertiser side of the formula outweigh the negative potential under the conditions (and fish activity level) you are faced with at that particular moment.

On the other hand, inactive bass might ignore a totally natural presentation (even if it's live bait), and startling them with something outlandish might be the only way to get any response at all. Even if your lure is a perfect representation of food, if the fish isn't interested in feeding, it probably won't respond. You won't get many bites with an unnatural presentation in a situation like this, but when the going is tough, few is major-league improvement over none.

Being forewarned that the various lure design factors can be negative, positive or unimportant in different situations or as a part of a different total IDP, anglers should be aware of some general presentation selection guidelines. There are many anglers' theories about aggravating bass, annoying them into striking, teasing them or forcing them to protect their territories. But other than hitting them during the spawn, getting a lure into the mouth of a bass is most often accomplished by making the bass mistake it for a potential meal. Most bass fishing should be designed around capitalizing on the predatory nature of bass.

This is not as difficult as it might seem. In the course of its normal feeding activities, a bass attempts to eat, or at least grabs and then quickly rejects, numerous items that are not actually

Complete Angler's Library

Bass are opportunistic feeders and will often grab an "easy meal" even if their stomachs are full. This 2-pounder had a partially digested 6-inch bass in its gullet; yet, it went for a large, slow-moving crankbait.

food. Because bass have no hands, the only way they can pick something up to get a better idea of what it is, is with their mouths.

How well the bass in its typical habitat can identify the real thing without getting a jaw-lock on it first is debatable. Obviously, the water clarity, the bass' activity level and the specific feeding situation all play a part; however, don't overlook the fact that most of its natural prey are well camouflaged. A successful predator must respond to cues if it is to eat regularly—a hint of movement, a glimmer of reflection, the subdued movements of something alive that's trying its best not to be noticed. All but the most dormant bass will strike something within its strike zone if positive triggers outweigh the negative ones. But show a bass too much of your lure, and you may increase the chances that the bass will recognize it as a phony before making a commitment.

The importance of proximity as a strike trigger cannot be overstressed. In most cases, the closer you can put a lure to a fish, the better the chances that the fish will respond to it. Make it easy for the fish to grab your lure and, usually, it will be more difficult for the fish to pass it up.

The advantages of proximity are easily recognized, but too often poorly executed. A modicum of casting accuracy is a must for the serious bass angler, but there is more to getting your lure close to fish than simply placing it next to a stump or into a tiny opening in the weeds. The really valuable skill is precision in controlling the lure. That includes accurate placement of the cast, followed by careful maneuvering of the lure as it moves underwater.

Proximity can play a major role in a broader-scope presentation characteristic called "ease of capture." To cook up a presentation based on this powerful IDP, add duration to the stock provided by physical proximity, mix in a measure of helplessness and a pinch of disorientation. If you leave out any unnatural ingredients, it's a stew that means trouble for all but the least active bass.

By repeated experience, bass learn what is easy to catch and what isn't. Eventually they learn, for instance, that something close requires less effort and offers a better chance for a positive result than something farther away. They also learn that an injured, dying or otherwise disoriented baitfish is less likely to escape than a healthy, alert baitfish. They don't know these things automatically, but the more feeding attempts they make in their lifetimes, the more information they acquire. A bigger bass, being an older fish, is a "smarter" (more experienced) feeder. It's not as likely to make the mistake of wasting energy trying to capture prey that's not easily caught.

Change Of Action/Speed/Direction

A sudden change in the speed or direction of a moving lure or in the way it flashes and vibrates—an instant IDP overhaul—often results in a strike from a bass that had been just following the lure. On occasion, a nearby bass that had shown little or no interest in the lure might even react to such a sudden change. This kind of fairly predictable response may be partly the result of simple reaction. *Surprise* may be a human term, but sudden reaction to surprising events is a basic instinct, certainly within the realm of the nervous system of a bass.

However, the sudden change in IDP may go beyond merely taking a bass by surprise. These unnatural movements might easily be interpreted as a sign of weakness or susceptibility, bringing the injured prey factor—which could well be the single most powerful strike generator available to us—into play.

When forage is abundant, serious anglers will turn to an IDP that mimics injured prey. Soft stickbaits imitate this strong strike generator while having few negative triggers that might turn bass off.

Erratic or unusual movement by real prey or by your imitation seems capable of drawing a vicious attack from a bass that might not otherwise expend energy to capture a meal. Perhaps such a reaction is nothing more than experience. Fish that have found injured prey to be an easy target in the past are likely to repeat the action.

It could go even deeper than that. Nature has no sympathy in its self-husbandry, and the law of the jungle applies equally to the aquatic community. In a world where "survival of the fittest" is the rule governing the overall health of the entire symbiotic eco-system, the weak and injured serve little purpose and are quickly culled; predators seem to respond aggressively to such individuals.

If you've got your yellow highlighter handy, this is the section you want to mark. Erratic lure action is the single most effective tool for raising the aggression level (and correspondingly, the

The well-detailed "naturalized" plugs catch bass; however, it is probably in spite of the detailing rather than because of it. Bass rarely identify their prey fully before a strike.

catchability) of bass. Erratic lure action is a positive trigger.

Prey Match

It has long been apparent to anglers that mimicking natural prey is one of the most effective ways to get a bass to take a lure. This has led to some incredibly detailed reproductions of natural food throughout the history of lure-making. But, in general, lures that are reasonably close approximations of the real thing are usually more productive than those that attempt a totally accurate representation.

Often, a lure's effectiveness is sacrificed or compromised in efforts to duplicate natural prey perfectly. More often, though, the problem lies with a difference between the angler's perception of reality and how the bass interprets what it sees. Humans see detail and often overemphasize it. The bass sees general shapes, colors and motion. The exaggerated scale and gill patterns popular on crankbaits in the early '80s are a good example. It's questionable whether a single bass ever recognized those imprinted and painted lines as scales, and bit a plug it wouldn't have, as a result. On the other hand, it may just be that the more detail added to the crude representations of nature, the more potentially negative cues that are being transmitted to the bass.

Unnatural Appearance

How can an unnatural appearance (or action) be a positive factor in lure presentation? One need only look at the typical spinnerbait to realize that a fish must either have a strong ability to ignore the fact that it doesn't look like anything it's ever successfully eaten, or must actually be triggered by the lure's totally foreign appearance.

It all goes back to the nature of the bass as an opportunistic predator. If it is on the prowl for food or waiting to ambush prey, it is keyed to respond not to the specific IDP of a particular prey but to anything that might be food. If something of edible size that's apparently alive (as evidenced by movement, flash and vibration) comes along, the bass simply reacts to it as a potential meal. It doesn't need to recognize it as a specific food item, so long as the bass doesn't consider it a non-food item. Unnatural-looking lures, being foreign to the fish's environment and experience, are unrecognized. Until it learns differently, the predatory bass often interprets anything that falls within the general size range of prey to be a possible meal, even if the bass doesn't recognize it. If it appears easy enough to capture, the bass usually will react to it. A spinnerbait in motion doesn't present much in the way of clues to its identity, and is really a "see-through" lure. The spinning blades cause intermittent flashing, but are not a solid target. The pulsating skirt is more of the same, but with a different appearance and color. In fact, its inconsistent IDP makes it difficult for a bass to correctly identify a spinnerbait. Still, on heavily fished lakes where spinnerbait use is widespread, bass do learn to avoid or ignore the most commonly used spinnerbaits. That's why every time a new blade configuration is produced, it's a hot item for a while. Using a willow-leaf blade instead of an Indiana blade can change the overall IDP of the lure enough to mask the appearance of a bait that older, more experienced bass may well have learned to avoid.

Because bass key on subtle clues, motion and vibration, simply using a standard lure with a nonstandard method often can put it into this category. On waters of the Chesapeake Bay, where the spinnerbait is the predominant bait, for instance, Ken Cook used a unique spinnerbait retrieve—a constant shaking of the rodtip—to move the lure in 6-inch spurts without making the blade turn. He won a Bassmasters Classic tournament. A year earlier, Rick

Clunn had accomplished much the same feat, winning the Classic by using a crankbait in a situation where almost any experienced bass angler would have used a spinnerbait. By giving the bass something that they don't recognize, almost anything can become a positive trigger.

Shape

Serious bass anglers need to consider several aspects concerning lure shape. One is the lure's visible profile. Is it long and slender, or short and bulky? Is it shaped like a minnow? A crayfish? An eel? Or like a sliver of metal and some wire and hooks? More importantly, what does its shape appear to be to the fish as it moves through the water?

Few lures have caught more bass than the slender minnow plugs represented by the Rapala models and the in-line spinner lures like those produced by Mepps. Both types effectively imitate minnows. One is shaped very much like a minnow, and the other looks absolutely nothing like a minnow. But in use, both are a representation of a minnow—or more accurately, something that might be a minnow. The Rapala-style lure works well when twitched along the surface. A bass can come up underneath it, zero in on it with its binocular vision, and still mistake the nearly motionless bait for a baitfish. The in-line spinner, on the other hand, relies on movement to disguise its unnatural shape. A bass sees the intermittent flash, recognizes it as a cue that it associates with prey and homes in on it. That the fish never gets a good look at it doesn't matter—a bass rarely gets a good look at many of the things it eats.

A lure's shape also affects its water resistance. A wide, bulky lure must displace more water in order to move. In doing so, it creates an abundance of displacement vibrations in the water, advertising its presence by alerting the bass through its lateral-line, vibration-detection system.

With any given style of lure, there will be times when a slender profile lure seems to strike the right chord with bass, and times when a bulkier bait seems to draw more positive responses. In fact, with jig-type lures in particular, body shape—the overall visible profile, not the exact shape—may be more important than tail action, color or any other element of the lure's design. When bass are hitting short, bulky grubs, slim, 4-inch worms may not be ef-

A lure with a generalized prey profile and low-impact colors, such as this plastic crayfish, often is much more effective at imitating natural prey than the more colorful and detailed lures.

Triggers And IDP

fective, and changing to a different color or tail-style of worm isn't going to change matters. Although bass might respond equally well to a jig-and-pig combination and a plastic worm on the same day, there are also times when the short, bulky jig will out-produce a long, slender worm hands down. And, there are times when the reverse is true.

Size

Everyone has heard that "big baits catch big bass," and it's of-ten true. Big baits catch big bass because bigger bass can eat larger prey. It's not a matter of them not responding to small baits, but one of smaller bass not responding to larger baits as frequently. In the typical bass environment, there are far more small bass than big bass, and because big bass (at least in the case of largemouths) often use entirely different habitats than small bass, patterns de-veloped for catching lots of bass tend to steer anglers away from big-bass territory. To a certain degree then, chances of catching big bass can be enhanced by not using lures that catch many small or average-sized bass.

In most cases, lures that create an IDP outside the normal-size range of bass prey are either ignored or, if intimidating and placed extremely close to the bass, can be negative triggers. Because ap-propriate prey-size range extends further on the large side of the scale for large bass, a negative trigger for an average-sized bass might be a positive trigger for a lunker. Very small bass, on the other hand, may not have enough experience to recognize out-sized prey as being difficult or impossible to catch and eat. Often they will strike their own size or larger.

Lure size is, of course, a far more important factor in the IDP equation when fishing for bass that are keying on specific prey rather than for ambush-oriented bass that are lying in wait for a meal. If a hundred bass are congregated in an area to take advan-tage of a school of 2-inch-long baitfish, a few bass might respond to a much larger lure while a lure the same size as the bait they are attacking could catch fish consistently.

Color

There are situations in which other considerations come into play in color selection. In bed fishing, as well as when fishing with floating worms, soft stickbaits and jerkbaits, it's to your advantage

For clearwater bass, a metallic-finished plug with its intermittent flash in the water is often a very effective positive strike trigger.

to use a bright, unnatural-colored bait if fish are aggressive. The simple fact that the bright color—bubble-gum pink or "hunter orange," for example—is easier for the angler to see in these shallow fishing conditions can be a major advantage.

A high-visibility stripe painted on the back of the slender minnow plugs used for ripping, jerking or even surface twitching has almost no effect on its fish-triggering capabilities because fish almost never see the back of these lures. However, it makes it much easier for the angler to guide it around cover, and fish it effectively.

Whether it's a hot-pink stripe on the back of a Rapala, a bubble-gum-colored Slug-Go or a fluorescent yellow tube bait being allowed to settle in a bed, it can serve as an effective strike indicator as long as the high-visibility color isn't turning off the fish. When the colored back disappears, set the hook!

Triggers And IDP

Intimidation

Large, aggressive bass might try to eat almost anything, but in moving down the scale of aggressiveness, the maximum size of potential prey also decreases. A large lure, especially one that moves aggressively itself, can intimidate a bass or make it react as if it were threatened. While bass are near the top of the food chain in most North American waters, every one of them started life much smaller, and consequently, much lower on the food chain. They would never have survived to adulthood without the instinct to flee or hide from anything threatening, and there is no reason to suspect that they don't retain those instincts.

This is especially true when a lure suddenly appears "out of nowhere." The same bass that would instinctively strike a small lure that appears suddenly might dart away or go deeper into cover if the sudden intruder were half its size.

Nowhere is this kind of reaction more evident than in flowing water environments. Small lures that don't approach from the normal, upstream direction may be ignored, or might even get bit. But a larger lure, especially one moving with a purpose like a heavy jig plummeting toward bottom or a big, deep-diving plug swimming aggressively upstream, suddenly entering the fish's zone of awareness from an unnatural position, can only be interpreted as threatening.

Depending upon a fish's activity level and on the clarity of its environment, objects with a blatantly unnatural IDP can easily fall into the negative-trigger category. Earlier, a spinnerbait's capacity to draw strikes despite its unnatural appearance was discussed. That is a matter of a spinnerbait's appearance being obscured by a barrage of undefined natural clues. The same spinnerbait lying on the bottom, with the clues provided by a whirling blade and pulsating skirt killed by lack of motion, becomes a pile of rubber, wire and shiny metal. Negative clues all the way.

However, a semi-transparent, dull-colored, soft plastic grub in a similar state of repose could easily be interpreted as a likely meal. So little is identifiable by the fish as possibly unnatural or threatening that the fish probably will treat it as prey. How it would respond to prey in that situation, of course, depends upon whether it is active and feeding, or in a neutral state.

Fish activity level is an important aspect when determining which side of the triggering scale lure visibility falls. Because most

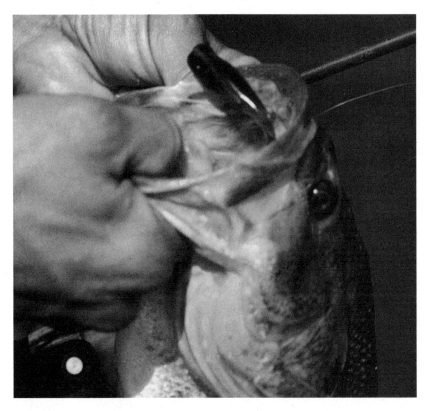

When bass fishing gets really tough, anglers find that it's difficult to beat the subtle, almost triggerless IDP of a well-placed smoke grub. Like natural prey, it's almost invisible and does little to advertise its presence. However, it must be fished close to the bass.

natural prey blends in with its environment, high visibility is inherently unnatural. But its advertiser qualities can, and often do, outweigh the negative aspects of an unnatural appearance. Just remember that active fish strike such lures in spite of, rather than because of, their high visibility color schemes. When the bite gets tough, trading away some advertiser qualities to remove the negative impact can be an important adjustment. This can be a factor with lure color, size and vibration values.

Speed

Fish can be caught on lures that move as fast as line can be cranked with a 7-1 ratio reel, as well as on lures lying motionless on the bottom. The speed at which a lure moves can have a major impact on its effectiveness in various situations. The correct speed can be an effective positive trigger. But there is usually some type of trade-off involved. The often-opposing factors of exposure duration and presentation efficiency must be taken into account.

The correct speed can be critical when trying to convince a bass that a lure is something real. Conditions that put baitfish and other underwater creatures in a state of reduced activity should be approached with presentations that work effectively at speeds appropriate for that activity level.

When bass are bunched up, as in winter's cold-water conditions, a slow speed approach is also a high efficiency approach. Keeping a lure in their midst is more efficient than repeatedly casting it to them. But when they are inactive and scattered, it usually still pays to trade the efficiency of a more up-tempo presentation for the effectiveness of the correct speed for the conditions.

On the other hand, some conditions call for a higher speed approach for more important reasons than simple efficiency. When water temperatures are higher, most aquatic creatures, especially from the middle of the food chain up, move faster and more frequently. During the early summer when food is most abundant, predators like bass can afford to be more selective, and may examine closely a potential meal that's not moving quickly before trying to eat it. The longer bass watch it, the greater the opportunity that something about the lure or the way you work it will strike a negative chord. That means the greater the chance that they may never grab it. At such times, an up-tempo approach can offset some of the negative triggers that are inherent in any artificial-lure presentation. The bass has to react immediately, or the opportunity is gone. This is a classic case of "the more fish you show it to, the more likely you are to get a bite."

Another factor in regard to speed as a trigger comes into play when fish are in between moods and seem willing to respond to a moving bait, but they are not quite energetic enough to really attack it. Typically, this is when fish will be striking short at a spinnerbait or bumping a crankbait half-heartedly. Instead of hanging a trailer hook on the spinnerbait and sacrificing snag resistance in an effort to hook those short strikers or changing crankbait colors in hopes of finding something they seem to bite more aggressively, try stepping up the tempo. Use speed to force them to react more aggressively, or not at all. Typically, when this approach works—which it almost always does on those days when all the fish seem to be striking short—you will get fewer hits with the higher speed approach; but, you'll hook the hits you do get. Obviously, this is a big improvement over getting more frequent bites but not landing any fish.

Somewhat related to speed are the factors that might best be called illusion of movement and sense of purpose.

The illusion of movement can include things like the wobble of a crankbait or the rippling action of a curlytail plastic worm or grub. A crankbait with a wide, slow wobble doesn't appear as energetic as one with a tight, brisk vibration. Unquestionably, fish react to one style of action more readily than the other at various times, and there are instances when any wobble or vibration is enough to turn fish away.

The same is true for plastic worms. Some designs have a gentle, flowing action while others give the illusion of something expending considerably more effort. Worms with a curled tail are more subtle than those where half of the body consists of a thin-curved membrane of plastic. And, of course, there are straight and flat-tailed worms to add to the mix. Short, thick, straight-tailed worms glide along smoothly, adding very little illusion of movement. Under low activity conditions, this kind of action is more in tune with what's going on underwater. Flat-tailed worms, depending upon the size and thickness of the tail section, as well as the segmentation of the body and the consistency of the plastic, move through the water with anywhere from an energetic, tail-beating motion to a supple slinking action.

Generally speaking, the slower the worm is presented, the less energetically the tail will move. A curlytail design used in a situation that calls for extremely slow movement and even zero speed application is, almost without exception, less effective than a straight- or flat-tailed worm. If its tail is thin and supple enough to work at such speeds, it gives a contradictory clue to the speed at which the lure is actually moving. More often, though, the tail doesn't do anything because it is set into action by water resistance as it moves. A plastic worm or grub sitting stiffly in a sickle shape as it nudges its way intermittently along the bottom is not going to be anywhere near as natural looking a bait as a flat- or straight-bodied lure would be in the same situation.

In a similar vein, a jig's rubber or the assorted flexible appendages of a plastic bait with "legs" can add a touch of motion—and

The IDP offered by small plastic worms makes them one of the most effective lures when bass are in a non-aggressive mode.

the illusion of life—to a stationary lure. The slight blur for a second or two of activity from the skirt or legs of such a "creature" after it settles to the bottom can be a powerful addition to a reality-based presentation. It can also help camouflage unnatural aspects of the lure's appearance.

Sense of purpose involves not only the speed of a lure, but its direction and steadiness as well. To understand this part of lure design, simply compare the action of two identical plastic worms—one rigged with a ½-ounce slip sinker and the other with ⅛ ounce of lead. The first appears to dive to the bottom as it sinks. The other drifts down aimlessly. Sense of purpose! One appears to be headed somewhere, the other doesn't. Fish recognize the difference.

Now imagine two identical 4-inch plastic worms—one rigged on an ⅛-ounce jig head, the other on a small, light-wire hook, trailing a foot or so behind a No. 5 split shot which happens to weigh just about what that jig head does. Both sink toward the bottom at the same speed. Both can be worked ever so slowly and gently across a gravel flat. But while one prompts a positive response from the bass, the other may be ignored. The worm on the jig head follows its nose, so to speak, in a hopping and diving manner. The split-shot rig, on the other hand, separates the worm from the weight's up-and-down movement. Instead of hopping and diving or crawling along the bottom with its nose down, the split-shot rigged worm swims and glides independently of the weight. In murky water, the jig worm will usually outproduce its shot-rigged twin. In clear water, the opposite happens.

Combinations of triggers and trigger values are the tools the angler has at his disposal to tune presentations to draw the desired

A plastic worm rigged to a lightweight jig can be a deadly combination for taking bass. The worm moves with a hopping, diving motion that is especially effective when used in murky water. This rig appears to have a sense of purpose.

Disturbance caused by a buzzbait not only helps to advertise the bait's presence but it also tends to mask the bait's unnatural appearance. This type of trigger encourages bass to take the bait despite its possible negative appearance.

response from the bass he hopes to catch. But there are so many factors, and so many variations of values for each of those factors, that you can't simply start from ground zero. Take advantage of every hint as to where to start, which design elements and presentation techniques to concentrate on and which direction to make any adjustments in. Fish activity level and aggressiveness are important. The types of prey the fish focus on in any specific environment are important. General environmental conditions in the waters being fished are important, as are the current weather and water conditions.

Although appropriate presentation IDP is important, it's all academic if you aren't fishing locations inhabited by fish. All aspects of lure design and performance are rendered neutral if there are no fish present to respond to them. In practice, that often results in the necessity for compromise, as habitat conditions impose limits on the choices of lures.

Any lure is a tool. To accomplish its job, it must be capable of getting near the fish. Deep-diving plugs must be chosen on how deep they dive. If they are not deep enough, the fish will be passed over—unnoticed or ignored. If they are too deep, you might be just burying the plug in cover and ruining the presentation. Snag-resistant lures are needed to fish in heavy weeds, timber or brush. Jigs must be heavy enough to reach the bottom in a high wind. All of this and more must be accomplished without losing sight of the IDP projected by the lure you choose. Within the parameters defined by the cover, depth and position, an angler must have an assortment of lures that span a wide range of IDPs.

19

Environmental Impact On Presentation

Determining the likely feeding attitude of the bass based on its position is important in selecting a lure to fish any specific situation. Changing lures to fit the probable mood of bass that might be using a specific spot can be a royal pain—especially if it's only for a few casts. An angler has to take cover, water color and other variables into account. This must be done to get a lure that works effectively, and to achieve just the right blend of advertiser and strike-generator qualities to appeal to the expected activity level of a bass that is likely to be using that spot and position. However, not making that extra effort is lazy fishing. And lazy fishing is dumb fishing. Why throw something that's not likely to draw a response from an inactive bass into a spot that's likely to hold inactive bass, or waste time trying to tempt a hesitant bass from a position that is more likely to be occupied by bass that are feeding and ready to grab the next available meal? Worse yet, why bother casting something that has little chance of working cleanly and effectively through the cover, or reaching the depth of the spot you're probing simply because the lure happens to be tied onto the rod you're using?

Cover

The type and density of the cover that you're fishing has obvious implications regarding the presentations that you'll be able to use. First and foremost, you must use a lure that is capable of performing in that particular cover. It's also important to use a

When cover is a major factor, as it was here, the angler has to carefully select a lure that will perform effectively in the cover, while still maintaining an effective IDP to trigger a strike.

Environmental Impact On Presentation   197

lure that will entice bass to respond positively. The cover the fish use and where they position themselves within it tell a lot about the way those fish are feeding. This type of information can help the angler select the right presentation.

A Texas-rigged plastic worm, for instance, will perform in almost any kind of cover, meaning that it can be pulled through it with relative ease. But if it doesn't trigger the fish into biting, all you're getting is casting practice. Bass riding high along the outside edge of a weedbed, for instance, can be reached with a worm—but you might have better success with running a lipless, rattling crankbait along the cover's outside edge. Their position tells you that they are active and looking to ambush passing baitfish. Conversely, if the fish are tucked into nooks, crannies and crevices within the cover, they probably are in a neutral to negative appetite mood. And opting for an up-tempo, horizontal approach would greatly hinder your chances of triggering a positive reaction, even though the lure works well in that cover.

Of course, practically speaking, you need a response from a bass or two in order to recognize their position. When possible, try to analyze how the cover lies before fishing it. Then, with the added information you gain with each cast, you can continue to adjust your techniques. When checking specific positions in and around cover, try using presentations that seem to be appropriate for the fish's probable feeding response, as well as for the cover's unique nature.

Fish that are "high and outside" are typically aggressive so check those positions with an up-tempo, horizontal approach. Rarely will a slow, methodical approach catch fish from those positions that a faster, less precise presentation wouldn't have caught, and usually in less time. On the other hand, fish that are tucked into crevices in cover—"low and inside"—typically are only slightly aggressive, and their response window is small. Rarely will a horizontal presentation trigger them. Select your presentation style based on the probable response of bass in the position you're fishing, as well as on the mechanics of dealing with the cover!

In the weed-fishing example described, when you decide to check farther into that cover, you've got several possibilities. For active bass farther into the weedbed, a spinnerbait or buzz bait may be ideal in sparse to moderate growth; if the vegetation is

A lure's negative triggers may be adequately disguised when it's fished in cover. However, this must be considered when the angler is fishing relatively cover-free areas where any negative triggers must be avoided.

thick, a weedless spoon or unweighted worm sliding across the top might be the better choice.

When trying to get to "non-chasing" bass deep in a weedbed, a Texas-rigged plastic worm works well. Yet, sometimes it's not the best choice! Sometimes bass respond much more readily to the shorter, bulkier profile of a jig and pork chunk, or the smaller and less intimidating size and action of a grub. It's always best to have a few options for each situation so you can offer an assortment of identity profiles to the fish.

Worming the bottom across a bed of moderate vegetation might best be done with ⅛ to ¼ ounce of bullet weight, or with a jig/worm, depending upon depth and weed density. Dropping it through holes in a surface-matted milfoil bed might be a job for ½ ounce of lead or more in order to put the worm on the bottom. If there are no suitable holes and you suspect that bass may be lying under the weed mat, try a 1-ounce bullet weight pegged to the line, and a short, straight-tailed worm. Make "rainbow casts" to send the worm crashing through the matted vegetation. It's not pretty, and you may spook some bass by giving them a quick-moving and unnatural looking lure. But there are times when nothing else will penetrate the slop.

For active/aggressive bass—even for neutral bass in some situations—a spinnerbait or soft stickbait will come through moderately dense weeds cleanly enough to get the job done. Meanwhile, it allows you to cover considerably more water than a worming or jigging technique. The soft stickbait, with its almost flawless, injured baitfish identity profile, seems to raise the aggression level of fish. The spinnerbait, on the other hand, by way of its built-in vibration and flash, reaches out into the awareness zones of more fish—especially in turbid water. Each has its strong points, and each is an exceptional tool for checking shallow cover for bass in neutral and aggressive moods.

Current

In a flowing environment, the current is simultaneously an enemy and an ally to the bass. It's an enemy in that it requires more constant expenditure of energy, and limits the areas in which a bass functions best. It's an ally in that it brings the food to the bass.

To the bass angler, the current is virtually all good news. Because it forces bass to work harder, it seems to build fish with more fight and energy. Current limits the usable areas so it narrows the areas an angler must search in order to find bass. And by acting as a natural food conveyor, it puts bass in predictable locations and positions so that presentation choices are simpler.

Nothing in bass fishing is absolute, but few axioms come closer than "bass in moving water hold in reduced current areas and face upstream." That's where their food comes from, and if you want to catch them consistently, that's where your lure should come from, too! River fishing for bass is almost always a matter of fishing either current breaks, current shear lines or current buffers.

In reading the current, you must learn to recognize the spots where bass will hold. Each cast must be planned in order to put the lure into the fish's awareness zone in a natural manner. For different lure types, different approaches are required.

Lures like jigs and plastic worms must be presented so that they flow to the fish. Lure weight and bulk must be balanced against the strength of the current so the lure can drift with the current as it sinks. Ideally, it will drift enough to look natural, yet still hold bottom fairly well once it gets there. This helps you take advantage of the duration/proximity trigger that's so important with jig-type lures. This is important when you drift a jig to the edges of the slack-water pocket on the downstream side of a current break where fish not actively feeding are likely to be present. Aggressive, active bass on the lookout for a meal are more often in the less well-defined pocket or pockets formed on the upstream side of a current break. Here, the view of approaching prey is less obstructed.

Surface plugs are surprisingly good lures in flowing water situations. This may be because the bass spend so much of their time in shallow-water feeding positions. However, casting to the likely fish-holding spots sometimes can be a waste of time. Not unlike jig fishing, surface plugging in the current requires planning. You must determine where to put your lure so it drifts to the fish. Then you use your rod to control—or at least influence—the drift's direction. Surface plugs are ideal for imitating an injured or disoriented prey which presses the aggression trigger. The idea is to make it look like a helpless baitfish struggling in the current. Again, the soft stickbait approach is one of the best injured-prey representations, almost certain to draw a fish response.

When they're fishing diving plugs and spinnerbaits in the current, some anglers will cast upstream and work the lure down-current in order to approach bass that are naturally facing upstream. But stop and think about this. If a comparatively powerful bass finds it necessary to face into the current, what direction do you suppose puny little baitfish face? A minnow, shad or perch struggling in the current is certainly not facing downstream.

On the contrary, it will swim into the current. Imagine a weak or injured baitfish struggling in the current, slipping backward each time it pauses. You can borrow a trick from West Coast salmon anglers who hold that diving plug in the current from upstream. The current works the bait, causing it to dive and wiggle. Let it fall back a foot or two toward a likely bass-holding spot, then bring it steady again. Pump it forward and let it fall back again.

Make it act like that struggling baitfish to entice strikes.

You can work a spot thoroughly and convincingly this way, and keep the plug in the fish's zone of awareness while making it act like an injured baitfish. If the current is swift enough, you can do the same with a buzzbait.

Water Color

Here water color is discussed as a normal environmental condition, not as a result of heavy runoff. A substantial difference exists between the two situations. One represents long-term conditions that the bass have had to adapt to, while the other is a temporary condition created by outside influences. The effects of these two conditions on the fish are totally different. So are the adjustments that anglers must make to catch them. (The short-term adjustments are covered in the next chapter.)

Even though bass can use all their senses in achieving their primary goal in life—feeding—they rely chiefly on the sense of sight. When you force them to rely on their other senses more by interfering with their vision, you put them at a serious disadvantage. Fortunately, other aquatic creatures are at a similar disadvantage in murky water as they attempt to avoid capture.

A bass angler's first reaction to murky water is usually to reach for brighter-colored, noisier lures. In situations where the water is normally murky, this could amount to overkill.

You can assume that bass residing in an off-colored environment rely heavily on their ability to detect underwater vibrations, both through their inner ear and through receptors in their lateral lines. That sense is more finely honed than it is in bass that live in a clearwater environment and can get along just fine with their sense of sight. In fact, studies have shown that bass taken from clear water, blindfolded and placed into a tank, repeatedly swim into the tank walls, while bass from a murky water environment don't.

Thus, selecting a louder lure to reach out to bass in an environment that is normally off-colored is a strategy akin to shouting so a blind man might hear you. It is not their hearing that suffers in the murky environment. So you can be certain that the prey the bass feed upon won't make extra noise so the bass can find them more easily. Everything that moves through the water creates displacement waves that a bass, especially one in a low-

Water color has a greater impact on lure selection than many anglers realize. When the water is murky, bass will locate their prey primarily by sound and vibrations.

visibility environment, can detect through its lateral line.

Scientists have found that the bass' lateral line is tuned to low-frequency vibrations which tend to be very non-directional. But the lateral lines, by way of their length and separation, provide a vibration-detecting sense that equates to binocular vision—or perhaps it is better equated with quadraphonic stereo sound. These vibration sensors give the bass directional/spatial information about vibrations and their sources. Along with its vibrational depth perception, the bass can actually distinguish speed and direction of movement.

Bass don't do this by thinking about it, just as a human doesn't have to think about the depth perception that comes with binocular vision. The human brain interprets the signals provided by two different views of the same subject from a few inches apart, and creates the impression of a single view with depth (distance) information. In bass, its brain interprets the signals sent by the vibration sensitive nerves in much the same manner.

If noisier lures aren't necessarily the answer, how can an angler best capitalize upon the bass' hearing and vibration detecting abilities? By using bottom- and object-contact, for one thing. Bump lures when you're fishing in murky water. The sound of the lure bumping on the bottom and into the cover helps bass locate those lures, but louder noise is not necessarily better. Experiment with sinker or jig-head weight to find the right combination.

Most anglers realize that in clear water, bass are more visually oriented. Typically anglers will opt for either very natural looking lures or lures that move so fast that the bass don't get a chance to see them as being unnatural.

Similar reasoning should be applied to vibrations in murky water. Bass in this environment are audibly oriented. Use sound/vibration criteria to choose lures that would equate to the visible appearance criteria used for clear water. Crayfish rustling around in the rocks may make "clicking" noises, but minnows swimming through open water certainly don't. Ideally, lures should either sound very natural, or they should be only loud enough to hint at their location and path.

In using color, the selection of bright-colored lures to increase visibility in murky water may or may not make sense. The importance of visual clues will vary considerably, depending upon the bass' activity state. In the case of truly aggressive bass, bright colors act much like vibrations: They help make a bass aware of the lure's presence, and any negative impact of the unnatural appearance is largely ignored. In the case of marginally active bass, however, the negative aspect of unnatural appearance may outweigh the "advertiser" qualities of increased visibility. The less active a bass is, the more likely the fish will interpret this lure design as being unnatural and perhaps intimidating.

Keep in mind that just as it doesn't make any extra noise in murky water, a preyfish doesn't take on fluorescent coloration, either. Often baitfish species—not unlike the murky-water bass themselves—do not develop the contrast coloration typical of clearwater creatures. This is because the need for natural camouflage diminishes in murky waters.

In recent years, chemo-reception which involves the senses of

When it comes to using scent-attractants, the author has done some testing of scents of his own on the water, as shown here. His tests indicated that the scent he was testing didn't make much difference in his catch rate.

smell and taste has been the target of much of the bass fishing industry's development efforts. Much has been said and written about bass and scent. Too often, it seems, catfish and, in some cases, trout and salmon are used as models, with the observations simply being applied to bass without any justification.

Bass do possess both olfactory organs and taste buds. Unlike catfish, bass taste buds are confined to the inside of the mouth—a physical attribute suggesting that the sense of taste is not often used when a bass hunts for food in low-light (or murky-water) conditions, as it would be in the case of catfish. Tests made to determine the effectiveness of chemical (scent) products used on artificial lures clearly illustrate that once a lure is inside the mouth of a bass, taste will determine whether the bass accepts or rejects it. Those same tests indicate just as clearly, though, that a strike is a

Environmental Impact On Presentation   205

In murky-water conditions such as this, anglers can't always depend on lures with scent- and taste-appeal to lure bass to strike. Lures with other positive triggers probably are a better choice.

reaction to visual clues rather than to chemical ones.

While there are claims that the olfactory organs are better developed in large bass than in small bass, the difference in olfactory acuity is between adults and immature bass. It further suggests that the bass' use of olfaction has more to do with reproduction than with feeding.

If you're trying to convince a bass to hold onto your lure long enough for you to react, chemo-receptor-based triggers may hold an answer. If you're trying to entice a bass to take your lure under limited-visibility conditions, there is little justification for the assumption that scent and taste hold any answers.

Water Temperature

Because the metabolism of fish changes when the water temperature rises or falls, obviously the feeding activities of bass will slow as the temperature dips. A bass doesn't need to feed as often in cooler water. Thus, it can afford to be "picky."

Of course, "picky" may be too human a term to be applied here, but it does seem to describe the situation. With the bass' decreased activity levels, more aspects of a lure's identity profile more often will fall under the neutral- and negative-trigger heading.

The key to successful bass fishing in cold water is locating the fish; however, in order to capitalize on finding them, it is then a matter of presentation. As already indicated, bass in most environments bunch together into a very limited amount of underwater real estate when winter sets in. Catching them is a matter of presenting a lure to as many of them as possible. Considering their reduced metabolic rate, bass won't be moving much so it means getting the lure to them and keeping it there for as long as possible under those conditions.

Jigs which can be worked slowly and left motionless on the bottom for extended periods are by far the most productive lures in cold water. Vertical and near vertical presentations result in longer lure exposure if the holding area is in reasonably deep water (which is usually the case).

Lure appearance is not as important in this situation as in most others, simply because these fish are usually deeper than the level of light penetration, and are responding to the vibrations produced by the lure as much as anything else. This is not, however, a call for active, noisy lures. The rest of the food chain is in a state of reduced activity, too. The sounds of bottom contact and the vibration of pressure waves created by anything that displaces water as it moves through the water are enough to alert the bass to the presence of a lure.

Depth And Breaklines

The depth at which the fish are holding has a profound influence on the choice of presentations. If an up-tempo approach in shallow water is needed, a good choice would be a tandem-bladed spinnerbait or a lipless crankbait, depending upon the presence of cover. In the mid-depth ranges, that same up-tempo approach might translate into a diving plug in the appropriate size for the depth being fished, or for a heavyweight single spin with a small blade which would minimize lift while still utilizing the "baffle 'em with motion" cues embodied in all spinnerbaits.

An angler should know—within a foot or so—the normal running depth on a variety of different line weights of every crankbait in his tackle box. This allows him to select the correct tool for the job when the time comes. Little attention should be paid to the diving depth listed by the manufacturer—most published figures are extremely generous. Even if they weren't, it is much more accurate and educational for the angler to test it in order to get a feel for the depth that the plugs reach on the length casts normally made with the lines normally used. It helps to learn how much impact rod position and retrieve rate have on various plugs. There are surprising differences.

An "original" Bagley's DB-3, for instance, on a typical 75-foot cast, using thin-diameter, 12-pound-test line (.0128-inch diameter) with the rodtip held just above the water surface during the entire retrieve, will reach a depth of 12 feet after being pulled just about 15 feet through the water. It will stay at that depth until the angle of pull is at about 45 degrees, at which point it starts toward the surface. That means it is at its "running depth" for less than 50 feet of the 75-foot retrieve. Holding the rodtip 6 feet above the surface of the water reduces the running depth by less than a foot. But it takes the plug almost 20 feet to reach 11 feet, and it starts ascending more than 15 feet from the boat. The time in the fish zone has been reduced by 10 feet simply by just holding the rodtip higher.

Tie the same plug to 20-pound-test line (.02-inch diameter) and, under the same conditions, it reaches its maximum running depth in about the same distances; however, those running depths are 8 and 6.5 feet, respectively, for the two rod positions. This doesn't mean that thinner line is necessarily better for cranking— just that it lets the plug dive deeper more quickly. It does mean, however, that the angler can effectively control lure depth with the type of line used and, to a lesser extent, the height the rodtip is held above the surface.

Twenty-pound test would be the obvious choice for bouncing that DB-3 off treetops 6 to 8 feet beneath the surface. (This would be a more snag-resistant choice than a smaller plug on lighter line in this situation.) In order to clip the edge of a breakline 15 feet deep, the plug may have to be fished on 10-, or even 8-pound-test line with the rodtip underwater.

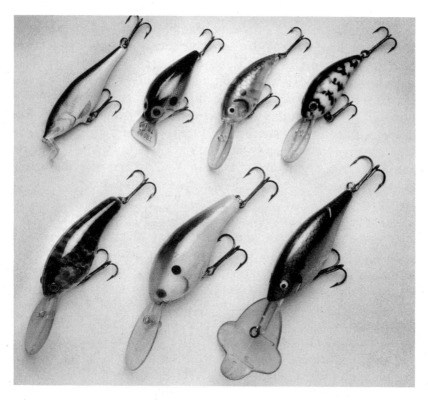

Forming a good crankbait selection are the two shallow-running minnow imitators (top row, from left) in 2- to 5-foot depths, two small deep divers (remaining lures, top row) for covering 5- to 8-foot depths, two full-sized divers (from left, bottom) and a magnum-sized diver for depths of 9 to 15 feet and beyond, respectively.

If crankbaits are fished a lot, it's wise to have not only a large enough selection of different models, styles and colors to cover the depths needed to check but a choice of suitable rods spooled with different-diameter lines, as well. This arrangement allows experimentation to find the best combination from a lure IDP standpoint while maintaining the necessary depth control.

Structure Contour

Bass that are using "low and inside" positions in cover are likely to be in a low state of activity and fairly sedentary. They aren't likely to move very far to gather in a lure, and they will be turned off by anything that's high in advertiser qualities. Precision placement of a "low impact" presentation is a must for catching these fish.

Precision presentation means getting the lure right next to the fish—or at least to the fish's probable location. Low-impact presentations mean lightweight, slow-moving, low-visibility lures with minimal advertiser characteristics. The problem that arises is that lures of this genre can be difficult to get into the crevices and tight, inside corners where these bass hang out—at least with conventional fishing methods. When you cast a jig or plastic worm—any type of sinking lure—it has a tendency to ride the line tension toward you in an arc as it sinks. It is physically impossible to make a lure sink straight down on a tight line, except from directly overhead.

If the spot being checked is deep enough, or the cover over it heavy enough, it's possible to vertically drop a lure. But in most typical cases—in 5 to 15 feet of water—vertical fishing is not viable; however, ignoring everything you know about jig and worm fishing is. Specifically, this is about letting the lure sink on a completely slack line. Not semi-taut. Not "controlled slack." Complete freedom to sink unhindered by the pull of the line.

Do not attempt to feel the lure sinking at all. Cast it or work it to the edge of the spot and drop the rodtip, extend your arms, even strip line off the reel if necessary to let it sink straight down. Don't fret about detecting the hit. You don't need to feel it, or even see the line jump. If a fish sucks a light lure on a slack line into its mouth, it's going to get the whole thing. A heavier lure on a tight line will pivot like a wind sock when the bass tries to "inhale" it, and, as often as not, only part of the lure ends up in the fish's mouth. The line tie and heavy head are still outside; sometimes, even the hook hasn't made it into the fish's mouth. The tight line relied upon in order to "feel" a bite better may be the reason for missing the fish.

Compare that to what happens when a fish does the same thing and there is no undue line resistance on a lightweight lure. The entire thing ends up in the fish's mouth. Remember, this is a fish that's not going anywhere. It didn't move anything except its mouth and gills to take the lure, and it's not going to swim away. After the lure has settled and you've allowed a reasonable length of time for a logy bass to notice and react to it, wind most of the slack out of the line, taking up the remaining bit by raising the rodtip with a finger on the line. If it feels the least bit heavier than expected, set hard and fast.

On days when there seem to be a lot of bass tucked tightly against the base of a drop or in the crease at the base of a weedline, use this approach and set "blind" on every cast, without even feeling for weight. It can be an effective, yet somewhat unorthodox, strategy.

Slack-line sink is used primarily to let lightweight, jig-type lures—whether hair jigs, plastic grubs or Texas-rigged worms—sink vertically into the nooks and crannies in which inactive bass so often hold. The hooking percentage is so high that once the technique is mastered you'll find yourself using it in more and more situations.

20

Outside Influences On Presentation

Weather conditions, as described through much of this book, will have a bearing on the activity level and position of bass. But because the influence is indirect and is based on the way the food source adjusts to these conditions, the impact may not be as predictable as anglers would like. Once the answer is worked out for a particular group of fish on a specific body of water at a particular time of the year, you can usually maintain contact with those fish through the changes in conditions. If an angler is observant and thorough enough in determining the relationships among predator, prey and habitat options in that body of water, that knowledge can usually be carried to other similar waters in which similar conditions exist.

In general, it's reasonably safe to assume that bright skies will find shallow residents holding tighter in cover. Cloudy skies, or any weather condition that limits or diffuses sunlight penetration into the water, will find fish roaming farther from cover in search of a meal. The weather's effects on the activity level and position of the bass obviously affects potentially productive presentation choices—slow and vertical for inactive bass pushed into concave structural configurations by bad weather, faster and horizontal for active fish under more favorable weather conditions.

Weather also imposes physical restraints on the angler's ability to fish effectively with certain available presentation options. By influencing how tightly bass use cover, the weather can also

212   Complete Angler's Library

Cloudy, pre-frontal conditions, such as this, will often result in increased bass activity because the fish will be less dependent upon overhead cover. Fish for these bass accordingly.

Outside Influences On Presentation

limit or expand the useable options. When it forces bass far under matted weeds, bright sunlight can effectively eliminate several hundred dollars worth of crankbaits in the tackle box from consideration, for example. Strong winds can effectively shut down fishing with light jigs, and by way of the chop they create on the water's surface, minimize the potential effectiveness of surface-oriented presentations.

Mechanical versatility, the ability to fish a wide range of presentation styles effectively, is the primary defense against changeable weather and water conditions. A situation that might call for a light jig and grub in normal weather conditions might best be fished with a vibrating metal blade bait or a jigging spoon in high winds. A chop on the water that makes fishing a Zara Spook an exercise in futility should send the angler to the tackle box in search of a slender jerkbait that works effectively near but under the surface turbulence checking for the same response from fish. The bass adapt, and so must anglers.

Fishing Pressure

In heavily fished lakes—all but the most remote places these days—fishing pressure can have a profound influence on the way fish act, especially on their responses to presentations. Combine a constant parade of artificial lures with the likely repeated exposure to the negative experience of being hooked, and you have to expect bass to get spooky. It's even possible that they can come to associate danger with the intermittent drone of an electric motor or the presence of a slowly moving boat in their home area. They either vacate the area or become inactive when those clues are present.

More frequently, though, individual bass learn to associate certain combinations of cues—specific IDPs—with the stressful situation of being caught. In confined waters with limited populations of bass, researchers have found that most bass quickly learn to avoid certain types of lures. Typically, after two or three experiences but, in some instances, after being hooked only once on a specific lure, bass began to show signs of avoiding the offending lure. Yet the same bass rarely learned to draw the same association with other lures and, in fact, were caught repeatedly on the same type of lure.

Obviously, the difference is one of lure identity. The more

easily identifiable a lure is—the more recognizable clues it projects—the more likely a bass is to learn to associate it with trouble. Soft-plastic baits and lures with no pronounced vibration seem to be particularly resistant to being "worn out" through constant exposure. The same is true of lower-visibility lures which have little in the way of an identifiable profile. An angler can approach the ultimate in "overexposure-proof" lures by leaning in the direction of small, straight-tailed worms in natural, translucent colors. Dull browns, greens and smoke tints, especially with black flake which helps break up the profile, blend in with the aquatic background and offer a bass little to identify. In that respect, they are far better imitators of most of what a bass eats than even the most detailed and perfectly sculpted artificials.

Does this mean that sooner or later, all high-impact type lures—those that emit loud vibrations with high visibility color schemes—will get "worn out" and will no longer catch bass? Hardly. Even bass that avoid a specific crankbait may hit other plugs without hesitation. And "learning ability" appears to be as much a factor of an individual bass' makeup as the lure's IDP.

Some bass never seem to learn. They seem to have a particular affinity for a specific set of triggers, and there's little that can stop them from reacting to it aggressively. It might be a spinnerbait, a particular crankbait or just about anything in the tackle box. Some fish are apparently suckers for a certain look or vibration.

In one national bass tournament held on the St. Lawrence River some years ago, one contestant weighed in the same fish on the first and third days of competition. (Tournament-caught bass were tagged prior to release, and this one had been fin-clipped by the contestant to visually separate it from his partner's catch in the boat's only livewell). This wasn't a young, inexperienced fish, either. It weighed over 4 pounds—at least eight years old given the short growing season of the Canadian-border site. The angler caught the fish at the same spot, three miles upstream from the weigh-in and release location on both days, and he caught it on the same crankbait.

Not many bass seem quite as anxious to get caught as that one did, but there are numerous recorded cases of the same fish being caught repeatedly—often on the same day—on the same lure. Be that as it may, there are just as many case histories involving fish that flee the area when a lure they've had a negative experience with comes into the territory. So anglers need to make adjustments when faced with a similar situation involving these "educated" bass.

How do you know whether the bass in any given lake have been "educated?" How often (and how long) do you have to wait in line at the launch ramp on a weekend morning? How many spots did you head to before finding one that was unoccupied the last time you went out on the lake? How often do you hang up on something— only to discover that it's another angler's broken fishing line? If the answer to any of these questions is "More than I'd like," you're fishing educated bass.

Obviously, the more time spent using low-impact lures—ones that blend with the natural environment rather than clash with it—the less there is to fight the bass' growing resistance to certain lures. But low-impact lures aren't always the answer to the conditions faced on the water.

Another tool in the battle to capture fishing-pressure-educated bass is to regularly use techniques that are outside the realm of normal. Although there are thousands of lures on the market, most anglers use pretty much the same narrow selection—not necessarily in brand name but certainly in function and IDP. When anglers focus on a certain lake or geographical area, the selection is even narrower. A lure gains a reputation for being hot and everybody on the lake uses it. Eventually, a list of "standard" methods for that lake, river or impoundment results. The fish are being exposed to the same group of IDPs over and over. Step outside the range of presentations that the fish are used to— without going too far outside the norm—and you're fishing for easier fish. Not like a virgin fishery, mind you, but certainly easier than trying to overcome a growing, population-wide immunity to a specific set of triggers.

Pay attention to what other anglers are using, and adjust your tactics accordingly. If the popular lures in an area are catching a lot of fish, join the crowd. But if the lake's developing a tough reputation, steer clear of the heavily used techniques and IDPs.

Look at the lures lining the walls of local tackle stores, leftover from the days when the lake attracted a lot of fishermen. Then devise an alternative as far removed from what most anglers have been throwing as you can. A somber hue instead of a bright one, a dead-slow approach instead of up-tempo, or vice-versa. If most spinnerbaits hanging in tackle shops or off rods in boats at the ramp are chartreuse with willow-leaf blades, choose black with a Colorado blade, or try burning a Rattletrap where most people would fish a spinnerbait. Change the program!

Stretch the list of acceptable presentations to extremes that most likely haven't been tried by the average fisherman. Most anglers tend to fish "by the book." Very few fish, though, have read the book. When the anglers who've been catching fish for years on a purple worm with glitter start to experiment, it's often limited to minor changes in that basic presentation. A grape worm with glitter, or blue with red flake. Go in there with a selection of lures that offers none of the clues associated with the previously hot technique, and you may have a field day. On lakes that have earned the "fished out" label, you can often trigger fish that pass up the usual offerings by going to the extremes in terms of lure color and lure speed. You may end up catching them, on a smoke grub, a white buzzbait, a shad-colored crankbait or a chartreuse Slug-Go.

Another aspect of fishing pressure to be considered is its influence on the bass population. To be educated, bass must escape or be released. While the catch-and-release ethic is strong among avid bass anglers, it is not universal, and it's not nearly as popular among the general fishing public as it is within the bass specialist fraternity. Many bass that respond to a purple worm or a white spinnerbait never get the chance to avoid that mistake again.

Putting It
All Together

21

Electronic Aids
For Finding Bass

Taking advantage of every opportunity to learn about bass and their environment is the cornerstone of intelligent fishing. The modern bass fisherman can use numerous electronic devices. He can, if desired, purchase depthfinders, horizontal scanning sonar and three-dimensional sonar, in addition to numerous electronic devices that measure the temperature of the water (at the surface and in the depths), the oxygen content, acid/alkaline balance and light penetration. Also, he can buy aerial videotapes of some of the most popular bass waters, as well as computerized fishing logs. All of these devices help anglers acquire and assimilate information about the fish, its habitat and its reactions to changes in its environment.

However, it's important to keep in mind that bass can be caught by an angler tossing a spinnerbait or topwater plug against the bank—without benefit of a single, space-age electronic marvel in the boat. Does that mean you should forgo electronic aids and rely entirely on your own wit and cunning? Hardly. The information provided by some of these devices is certainly too valuable to pass up.

Chief among these valuable tools, is a quality depthfinder. If you're a serious bass fisherman, you almost certainly have one on your boat, or possibly two or three. On the boats used by top bass pros, it is not unusual to see at least one flasher or LCD unit mounted at the bow, and another with either a larger, more complex LCD or a paper-graph recorder on the console. Each unit

Most bass anglers wouldn't go fishing without a depthfinder, and many have several. A modern bass boat would not be complete without a unit placed near the tip of the bow. Quite often, the transducer is attached to the lower stem of the electric trolling motor.

Electronic Aids For Finding Bass

serves a specific purpose with a combination giving more complete coverage.

A unit that gives a very detailed picture of the underwater terrain, as well as fish, schools of baitfish and possibly even the thermocline is a major advantage. This "detail" unit serves as underwater eyes in searching for potentially productive areas, and in learning as much as possible about what's available in terms of habitat.

Because this sonar unit is primarily for exploring and searching, a unit that provides broad bottom coverage is advisable. Bottom coverage is, of course, determined by the signal-cone angle. The key factors are the operating frequency and transducer design. Some manufacturers rely on one method, while others choose the other to control cone angle. In general, though, a cone angle of 30 degrees or more—whether resulting from a low operating frequency or a wide transducer—is desirable for use on the console-mounted unit.

Sonar that shows tremendous detail takes some degree of concentration to use. If for no other reason than safe navigation, a separate, console-mounted unit showing limited detail, yet extremely easy to read for determining depth is almost mandatory. The two should operate at different frequencies in order to prevent interference.

The transducers for the two console-mounted units must be mounted properly to ensure that they work with little or no interference when the boat is running at least at cruising speed. The "safety sonar" must be capable of being read reliably at any speed. This is usually best accomplished on single-hull, fiberglass boats by bonding the transducer to the hull inside the sump area. Transducers should not be mounted inside aluminum boats, however. Some sonar experts also mount the "detail" unit's transducer internally while others insist that too much signal strength is lost passing through the hull and demand an on-the-transom, external mount for this transducer. Most top-of-the-line sonar units also read the speed and the surface temperature so their transducers must be mounted externally, anyway. Obviously, installation of any unit should be a "no compromise situation. (More detailed information about installing and operating depthfinders can be obtained by reading the Complete Angler's Library book, *Fishing With Marine Electronics*.)

This angler has his depthfinders close at hand so that he can continue to monitor fish activity and structure as he fishes from the bow of his boat. This gives him more precise control in identifying subtle changes that may be occurring underneath.

While the console-mounted depthfinders are the tools used for searching out potentially productive fishing areas and for analyzing the lay of the submerged land, the depthfinder positioned at the fishing position—normally the bow in a modern bass rig— serves another purpose entirely. It keeps the angler in contact with the structure and cover, and helps him find the subtle changes that fish key on while he is actually fishing. In contrast to the wide field of view that's preferred with the console-mounted unit, a narrow cone angle is better for this "precision" work. It's not unlike the difference between taking a photograph of the entire scene with a wide-angle lens and then zooming in, or switching to a telephoto lens to capture more detail.

For maximum benefit, the front depthfinder, with its front-mounted transducer, should be used in conjunction with a bottom-contact lure, combining visual and tactile exploration of the bottom. Most experts agree that the front depthfinder's transducer is best mounted directly on the trolling motor's lower unit. Some anglers, though, have discovered the advantage in increased information-gathering capability when comparing different views from a pair of transducers—one at each end of the boat—connected to the front unit via a switch. Others prefer to mount the console unit with its rear transducer-generated signal on a swivel, and rotate it when comparative views are desired while fishing. Those signals then are visible from the fishing position, and are to be used in conjunction with the front mount's data for analyzing the severity of drop-offs and the like.

But what kind of depthfinder will provide the best performance in the all-important "fishing position?" If you've bought a new depthfinder recently, odds are it's a liquid-crystal-style unit. LCD units are not capable of displaying the subtle differences in signal strength that flashers and paper graphs can. Instead, the built-in computer interprets the signal, and decides whether it is the bottom, weeds, a fish or whatever, and displays it accordingly. Unfortunately, neither that computer nor the man who wrote the program has tied on a jig and felt around the bottom of the lake that the operator is fishing.

But in today's world, most anglers use LCD screen machines. Relatively few people can effectively interpret the nuances of a flasher's display, so the automated features of the modern LCD units are likely to be more beneficial to people.

The better quality LCD units on the market today are capable of showing enough about the bottom for an angler to get a feel for what's going on under the boat. If you want to invest the time to gain that information (and you should), turn all the automatic features of the unit off. That includes autogain or power, autoranging and especially any kind of a "FISH ID" feature in which little fish shapes appear on the screen. If the unit has a grayline feature, turn it on.

After you have your boat in position in about 20 feet of water over a known hard bottom, increase the gain until you get a strong signal at 20 feet and a weaker, "double echo" line at 40 feet. Set up like this, the unit will show the bottom, the fish that aren't "nailed" to the bottom and the breadth of the "real" bottom signal. Combined with the presence of the "second echo" and its

A console-mounted depthfinder works well for marking a hump or other deep structure. Once the electric motor is in the water, a front-mounted flasher unit is indispensable for staying tight with the breakline.

strength, this will provide all the information you will need to know about bottom consistency in order to be successful.

Keep in mind that when you look at an LCD screen, you are not looking at a picture of what is under your boat. The farthest vertical row of pixels to the right edge of the screen shows you approximately what a flasher unit would be showing you, except that the information is arranged in a column instead of around a dial. The rest of the screen represents time, not location. Therefore, the screen shows the things that were under your boat the last 20 or 30 times the unit checked (depending upon the screen's width).

While it can be difficult to avoid looking at the middle of the screen when you're interested in what's under your boat right now, the only thing that matters is the extreme right hand edge of the LCD unit. The rest of the display is valuable for other reasons: It shows you things you may have missed when you had your eyes off the screen, and it helps you develop a feel for the contour of drop-offs and composition breaklines that even very experienced flasher users have a hard time achieving. But when you want up-to-date, flasher-type information, you have to remember to look at the right-hand column.

Electronic Aids For Finding Bass

Of course, if your depthfinder also has a built-in surface temperature gauge, that too can prove valuable—especially in the spring and fall. Measuring the surface temperature during the two periods of the year when changing water temperatures affect bass the most and signal the advancing seasonal changes can be an important aid in helping you to put patterns together on the waters you frequent. It can also be helpful in locating submerged springs (There is usually a few degrees difference on the surface over a spring.) and for ascertaining whether incoming water is warmer or cooler than the lake water.

As far as a temperature probe that can be lowered into the depths is concerned, the chief use for one in bass fishing is to determine the depth of the thermocline. But because the thermocline can be identified by the accumulation of particulate matter that builds up in it, it can actually be seen on a high-quality graph or liquid-crystal unit—without spending time lowering a probe over the side, reducing the value of the probes.

As far as finding a bass' "comfort zone" is concerned, they have a very wide range of temperatures at which they function just fine, and they do not suspect the existence of more "comfortable" conditions elsewhere if conditions where they are do not repel them. Time invested looking for a supposed "comfort zone" could be much better spent in other pursuits. The same can be said for oxygen meters and pH meters. They may help you to understand more about the environment and, thus, prove useful on a long-term basis. But as for finding fish on a day-to-day basis, there are far more effective ways.

The commercial device that measures light intensity and purports to tell you what color lure to use deserves special consideration. The fishing philosophy outlined here involves adjusting the presentation to the activity level of the fish. Lure color is an important element in presentation adjustments in that certain types of presentations, in certain situations, are dependent on minimizing unnatural triggers. It involves doing the best job possible to make the lure that's offered blend in with the bass' environment. Following the advice of a color selection device could be self-defeating in those instances. Because it measures only the intensity of light and not the color balance which is affected by water tint and the angle of the sun, it may not be able to accurately indicate even the most visible color. Water, after all, is rarely perfectly clear. It can be tinted green, reddish brown, gray or yellow; and different wavelengths (colors) of light pass through different colors of water at different rates, totally changing the value of the light and the visibility of various colors.

Just as taking time to learn about fish in various environments can help increase your ability to understand the interrelationships that exist, investing time to study other factors that less-advanced anglers would consider "unrelated" to the task at hand can be advantageous.

Fishing technology really takes a giant leap forward with the popularization of Global Positioning Satellite (GPS) devices. Although not directly related to finding fish, these instruments triangulate signals from "stationary" satellites to pinpoint locations. Big-water anglers have relied on loran instruments to help them return to productive locations for years. But loran's limited accuracy, along with the limited areas of coverage afforded by its land-based transmitters and repeating stations, did not make it a justifiable investment in the minds of many inland anglers. When the spot you need to mark is a 3-foot-diameter rock in the middle of a quarter-acre hump, getting within a few hundred feet isn't much of an advantage.

With GPS, however, the investment is larger, but the limited coverage and insufficient accuracy arguments are no longer pertinent. Even the most basic GPS units can lead an angler to within a few yards of his hotspot. At maximum sensitivity, GPS can tell you exactly where to vertical-jig your lure!

GPS technology isn't for every angler, and it may be a while before it's accepted as mainstream technology among inland fishermen. However, it's available today, and for those anglers who fish large waters where most of the fish use offshore structure, it is an attractive option.

22

Specialized Tools

Tackle that is high quality is, of course, a necessity. It is difficult to enjoy fishing and interpret conditions when struggling with defective gear or tackle that's not designed for what is needed to accomplish those purposes. But it's assumed that NAFC Members are not trying to make do with inferior gear. The emphasis here will be on maintaining a level of quality rather than recommending specific models. Still, there are certain tackle considerations that can make the style of fishing being discussed here a lot more effective.

Rods, Reels, Line

Because applying the right lure presentation to a specific situation is an integral part of this fishing philosophy, it is advisable to have several outfits of various "weights" on hand. Not only does it save a lot of time changing lures, but the correct rod and line for a specific application invariably make fishing that presentation easier and potentially more effective.

Every serious bass angler should carry at least one 6- to 8-pound-test outfit, one medium-range rod and reel spooled with 8- to 10-pound-test line, and one or more heavier-action rigs, carrying line of 12- to 17-pound test. Ideally, the angler will also have a special-purpose rod like a flipping stick, carrying some real rope—say, 25-pound test—for fishing dense cover, and a duplicate of the outfit that most suits his personal style or the conditions he most often faces. The line tests and appropriate rod actions specified will

Modern bass tackle covers a wide range of applications: from yanking bass out of heavy cover to easing a split-shot rig across a deep point. It must be durable enough for normal use, yet light and sensitive at the same time.

Specialized Tools

cover a wide range of conditions; however, they should be adjusted accordingly if the waters present unique situations.

If you regularly fish where huge fish in heavy cover are common, such as Florida, South Georgia and certain areas of Texas, you might consider moving everything up a notch or two—8- to 10-pound test on the "finesse" rod, 12 on the medium-action, 17 to 20 on the heavy-action casting rods and 30-pound test or heavier on the flipping stick. If, on the other hand, your usual fishing waters are clear and deep, like the Great Lakes or the impoundments of the far West, you would benefit from similarly scaling the line weights down to 4 to 6, 8 to 10, 12 and 17 on the flipping stick.

Can you catch fish with fewer than three to five rods? Of course. You can catch fish on a willow branch and a piece of string, too. But it certainly limits your versatility.

Every cast you make in this style of fishing has two purposes: to catch a fish, and to probe for additional information about the fishing conditions. The rod's ability to transmit information to your hand is its most important design feature. A few generalities about construction can help you in selecting the most sensitive tackle.

Unlike bass behavior, the laws of physics are predictable and inflexible. For example, the heavier an object is, the more energy it takes to move it. More vibration (movement) sent up the line from the business end (the lure) will reach your hand if it has less weight to move in doing so. This means that a rod weighing 3 ounces is inherently a better tool for feeling the bottom and for feeling bites than one that weighs 6 ounces, or even 3½ ounces.

The less motion lost in bending the rod, the more motion there is to reach your hand. Despite all you may have read and heard over the years about "light, sensitive tips" on rods, the stiffer the action of a rod, the more sensitive it is.

In general, from the perspective of being better able to interpret the signals sent up your line, use the lightest, stiffest rods you can cast effectively with any specific combination of lure weight and line size. You can't get away with 6-pound test on a flipping rod, but spinning rods rated for 6 are usually much too soft to effectively feel the bottom and the habitat conditions. Light, graphite rods rated for 8- to 12-pound-test line and ¼- to ½-ounce lures are usually much better tools for fishing ¹⁄₁₆- to ¼-ounce lures on

A lightweight, yet relatively stiff rod provides a better "feel" for what is happening down below. Vibrations telegraphed along the line are better felt by the angler if there is less rod weight to be moved.

Specialized Tools

6- to 8-pound-test line. The same reasoning should be applied up to the heaviest freshwater tackle.

Line selection itself is and will continue to be an area of controversy. There are two opposing views about line selection. One promotes choosing the heaviest line you can get away with under the conditions you're facing, while the other supports the use of the lightest line possible for the situation at hand.

For NAFC Members' purposes, the thinnest line providing enough strength and shock resistance for any specific application is the usual choice, except in certain narrowly defined situations. The reason is simple: Thin line has less water resistance so less of the signal is lost on its way to the rod. The copolymer, premium lines, being thinner per pound test than the best monofilaments, represent a major advance in fishing tackle.

The exception to the "thinner-is-better" rule is found in very heavy cover situations where the added abrasion resistance of thicker line comes into play. Actual abrasion-resistant qualities of the line aside, a nick or scrape 0.003-inch deep in line that's 0.01 inch in diameter is a far more hazardous situation than that same 0.003-inch nick in line that's 0.03 inch thick.

For that reason, then, in flipping situations and for weedless spoons, as well as in some spinnerbait applications, 25-pound-test line, or even 30-pound test in the thin-diameter style is often a better choice. These are applications, though, where the need for supersensitivity is minimized by the fact that you're either fishing the lure within eyesight (surface spoons, buzzing spinnerbaits), or you are operating on such a short line length (flipping) that reduced "feel" is a negligible factor.

Experienced fishermen recognize the advantages of fresh line. Most buy their line in bulk spools and replace the used line (the 75 to 100 feet you actually use to fish) every few trips. When you're buying in bulk, line storage becomes a factor. The proper way to store line and how long it may safely be stored are areas of considerable disagreement.

Monofilament line is made of nylon alloys; however, the copolymer and tripolymer lines that dominate the premium monofilament market have an assortment of related plastic compounds in their composition. Despite these variations, major line manufacturers all provide similar recommendations for long-term storage. Avoid heat and humidity. That means your car trunk and the

Improved Clinch And Palomar Knots

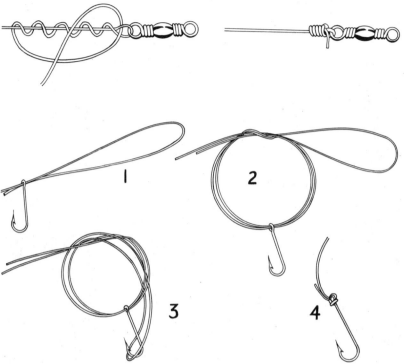

The two-phase illustration at top shows how the improved clinch knot is tied. Below are shown the steps used in tying the palomar knot. Both are recommended ways of attaching terminal tackle.

boat's storage bin are not suitable places for long-term storage. It also excludes the garage loft or a damp cellar—places where a lot of anglers store their equipment. Oddly enough, the most recommended place for line storage is the freezer! Yes, seal the line in zippered plastic bags and store them in the freezer.

Discussion of line naturally turns to knots. Most bass fishermen use one of two knots: the improved clinch knot or the palomar. With normal, nylon monofilament, either is adequate. With the modern, extra-thin copolymer lines, though, the palomar is superior. The improved clinch knot relies on compressing the line or distorting its cross section in its wraps to prevent slippage. The copolymers, however, gain their strength, limited stretch and increased abrasion-resistance qualities from a "hard" finish that resists distortion. Clinch knots tied with copolymer lines can slip easily unless clinched excessively tight—which "fractures" the finish resulting in a weak spot that's particularly low in shock strength. If you use these lines—and their advantages are very attractive, so you should at least try them—discipline yourself to always tie a palomar knot.

Lightweight, stiff-action rods coupled with lightweight, smooth-action reels and thin, low-stretch line allow more of the signals sent from your lure to reach your hand. They make the job of "fishing by braille" much easier and more effective. This is important to remember when selecting tackle. It's all about making it as easy as possible to gather as much information about the underwater world as you can.

Accessories

The most important accessory you can have is a pair of high-quality polarized sunglasses. As far as getting a first-hand glimpse —albeit a limited one into the shallowest portions—into bass habitat, the difference between wearing polarized glasses and not wearing them is astounding. The difference between top- quality, optical glass lenses and run-of-the mill lenses found on inexpensive glasses is nearly as great.

Top-quality polarized glasses are a sizeable investment. Choose wisely; they're worth every penny. While the lens color is affected by a person's preferences, maximum effectiveness under the widest range of water and weather conditions seems to bias the decision toward photosensitive, amber/bronze lenses. The amber/bronze tint seems to offer the best view into the water, as well as cutting through early morning mist. The photosensitive feature, in which the lenses darken reciprocally according to the amount of ambient light, means that they work equally well under both dim light and bright sunlight.

Lightweight, graphite-composite frames will minimize the headache which some folks get when using the heavier glass lenses. Side shields that prevent glare from entering from the sides of the glasses and being bounced off the inside of the lens are preferred over the contoured, "wrap-around" style lenses.

If you wear corrective eyewear, it's tough to find "clip-ons" in top-of-the-line lenses. A separate set of prescription glasses ground with polarized, photosensitive optical glass, or a good pair with effective side shields worn over contact lenses is a far more effective (but admittedly costlier) solution.

Other specialized tools that fit into the accessory category, include line-trimmers, a pair of decent quality long-nose pliers, some type of hook-sharpening device—either a file, stone or portable electric sharpener—and a set of marker buoys.

Used with your depthfinder(s), marker buoys are an invaluable aid in analyzing the underwater situation when you're fishing offshore drops, humps and reefs. A few strategically placed buoys provide "reference points" that not only make fishing the structure easier but make it possible to find the position of minor breaks (or fish).

Even with those reference points, however, many knowledgeable "deep-water experts" keep a spare marker buoy on the front deck, with the weight already unsnapped from its fastener, so it can be kicked overboard quickly to mark a spot precisely when the need arises. Obviously, the need often arises when you're busy fighting a fish and you want to mark your position. Just be sure to keep the fish on the opposite side of the boat from the marker as you fight and bring in the fish.

The Most Substantial Tool

Some bass fishermen seem to carry rods only as an excuse to ride around in a fast, sleek-looking, high-performance bass boat, while others view the modern bass boat as over-sized, over-powered and over-priced. But whether competitive fishing fits into your personal activities or not—even if you fish from a basic 14-footer—there's no denying that your boat is a better, more convenient and safer fishing platform because of design concepts that evolved directly from tournament-oriented bass fishing. Everything from level flotation and "kill switches" to livewells, adequate covered storage, front-mounted electric motors and raised casting platforms were derived from competitive bass fishing.

The right boat, properly equipped, can make fishing more enjoyable and more productive. But there's no universally "right" boat for all bass fishermen or all bass-fishing situations. If your bass fishing is limited to shallow, weedy ponds, a canoe or a 10-foot cartopper might be all the bass boat you'll ever need, and a lot more practical than an 18-foot, high-performance rig with enough equipment to outfit a small navy. On the other hand, if you fish moderate-sized natural lakes which present various conditions, and make an occasional trip to a larger reservoir, a 15- or 16-foot boat—either fiberglass or aluminum—with most of the accoutrements of a full-sized tourney boat can be a big advantage. If larger natural lakes or reservoirs are your primary stomping grounds, a fully equipped, "tourney-style" boat with enough performance to make the entire lake available to you at any time might be the best boat for your needs.

Remember, the purpose of the boat is to provide a stable and maneuverable fishing platform, and to carry all the gear you need for a productive trip. It should be chosen on how well it fulfills your fishing style, not on whether it's the latest model or the hottest thing afloat.

If you fish tournaments, for instance, a larger, more seaworthy boat offers numerous advantages, most notably the ability to travel a long distance safely, even in bad weather. The size and functionality of the livewell system also becomes a major factor in choosing the right boat for competitive fishing.

The non-tournament fisherman, on the other hand, may never even use livewells. Some even convert them into extra dry-storage areas or ice chests.

If most of the fishing in your home waters is shoreline-related, especially if the cover is heavy and flipping- or pitching-style presentations will prove advantageous, a boat with a large, raised front deck will make your fishing much more trouble-free and probably more productive, as well. If you spend more time fishing offshore humps or outside weedlines, especially if you prefer to sit down while fishing, the raised deck can actually be a hindrance.

Of course, no discussion of bass boats and other boats for bass fishing would be complete without a look at the electric trolling motors that are integral to the sport. Trolling motor, is, of course, a misleading name. In bass fishing, they're used to propel or position the boat while fishing, but rarely are they used for actually pulling a lure through the water, as in trolling. That's not to say, of course, that no one trolls for bass, or that bass can't be caught by trolling. But the electric motor on a typical bass boat is not often used for trolling. In fact, anglers who use effective bass-trolling techniques typically use smaller boats, and most likely troll with gas engines.

A bass boat's electric positioning motor must be strong enough to pull the craft into a stiff wind, and quiet enough to maneuver in

The modern bass boat is more than a water-craft. It not only serves as a fishing platform, but as a necessary tool that is integral to the serious bass angler's fishing success.

shallow, confined areas where noise is likely to spook or startle bass. It is usually mounted on the bow, although some anglers mount one at each end of the boat, providing more flexibility.

Using a foot- or hand-operated trolling motor is a matter of personal preference. While foot-operated motors grew out of the bass tournament scene, many, if not most, of the top pros opt for hand-controlled electrics today. The reasons given for this choice vary, but reliability and more precise control are the two most commonly cited. It's undeniable that the fewer the moving parts, the fewer things there are to break or malfunction. Few things are as frustrating as having a trolling motor steering cable break five minutes after you've started fishing, following a 20-mile run up the lake. Among non-competitive bass boat fishermen, however, foot-operated electrics dominate because many cite losing a fish while having to take a hand off the reel at an inopportune moment.

Optional setups include extended handles for hand-controlled motors bringing them within reach of the angler from their "way-out-front" mounting position, "kick" handles designed to allow hand-operated motors to be steered with the foot and deck mounted, foot-operated on-off switches for hand-operated motors.

Specialized Tools

Bass Lures

Everybody has a favorite lure or a lure in which they have utmost confidence. Something they know will catch bass if they can just get it in front of one. Difficult as it is, anglers should discipline themselves to avoid over-reliance upon "favorites." Lures should be viewed as tools and the tackle box as a tool box. Most spend too much time trying to get fish to respond to what they want to catch them on, instead of trying to figure out what the fish really want.

An array of lures in a typical tackle box should include the tools to handle every combination of habitat options available (depth and cover considerations). This should cover the spectrum of possible bass position/activity-state combinations associated with each of the habitat options encountered, along with an effective range of IDPs for each.

Rather than muddying up the mental waters with questions and decisions about different colors, specific sizes and so forth when probing for initial contact, use universal, or multi-purpose lures, and don't worry about fine-tuning the IDP until some sort of pattern takes shape.

Probing Lures

There has probably never been a lure that wouldn't catch bass at one time or another. The key is matching the lure to specific conditions including depth, cover (or lack of it), water clarity and the position and activity level of the fish. If it functions well for the conditions and carries appropriate triggers, it's the right lure for the job—at least close enough to get you started. Getting on track is important, especially when visiting new waters or waters you haven't fished in some time.

Early in the game, when the most important task at hand is learning where bass might be, use a heavier jig than you might otherwise use. It's usually one of the best tools for feeling the bottom and learning what's there. It might not be exactly what the bass will respond to most willingly, but it does help you find places that are worth spending the time to experiment with other weights, actions and colors.

A floating/diving plug can do double duty as a surface lure, at least for checking an option. If, in fact, something starts clicking with it, and there is surface activity, switch to a more appropriate surface plug, a buzzbait or perhaps a soft stickbait.

For purposes of investigating potential habitat, few lures are more versatile than a single-bladed spinnerbait. It will come through most forms of cover, can be fished as a "drop bait" as well as a with more or less steady, horizontal retrieve and can even be jigged along the bottom.

The same plastic worm that was rigged "Texas-style" with a ¼-ounce weight in order to snake through the branches of a submerged tree will effectively probe the depths of a cabbage patch. Without the weight, the same lure will swim enticingly across the surface of a matted milfoil or lily-pad bed. Switch to a heavier weight and a barrel swivel so it's rigged "Carolina style," and it's perfect for fishing a deep, stump-strewn point.

=23=

Some Assembly Required

Understanding how the bass' awareness zone influences fishing success has already been discussed. The angler's eventual success can also be affected (perhaps even more so) by another awareness zone—his own. Throughout this book one theme of overriding importance has been stressed: The key to success is understanding the bass and how it relates to its environment. That environment isn't limited to the water, the bottom and the weeds. It includes many other creatures that exist there as well. They are the critters that bass eat, the ones that compete with bass for food and even those that seem to have few, if any, direct interactions with the bass. The lake that is being fished, and nature itself, is a complex web of interrelated and interdependent entities.

The human intellect and its tendency to rely on its own cleverness rather than natural cycles and forces has insulated man from the everyday existence in the natural world. Thus, man lost the ability to feel nature's pulse many generations ago. Now, in an effort to understand that natural world, man must train himself to use his intellect to identify signs of that activity—a trait that ancestors-far-removed probably found instinctive.

Most anglers realize that a swirl on the surface or a flock of birds diving to the water for baitfish can indicate a potentially productive situation. However, few anglers act on it, other than to perhaps direct a half-hearted cast in the general direction of the natural clue. How many take into account the general activity

One of the major benefits NAFC Members gain from fishing is the opportunity to be a part of nature. Getting "in tune" with nature will increase fishing success.

level of bank-bound wildlife? Or note the cycles of insect hatches in relation to the barometer? Or pay attention to any of the many possible natural signs of life?

When anglers concentrate too much on casting prowess or any aspect of the task at hand and fail to notice the squirrels, rabbits, deer or whatever beyond the water's edge, they not only belittle the quality of their experience in the outdoors, but also risk missing natural clues that can make the job of catching fish easier. Wildlife is often prompted into higher states of activity by the same unseen and unrecognized forces that affect the fish. Keep your eyes and ears open, and try to get closer to nature's pulse without turning off your main advantage—the ability to reason and to discern logical connections and chains of events.

Anglers must also train themselves to visualize what the un-

Some Assembly Required

derwater world is like. While riding along a country road, note the land's contours. The hills, ditches, stone walls, gorges and flat valleys along the roadside are not all that dissimilar from the bass' world. Imagine the area inundated with water. Try to identify the spots that predators would use. Then imagine trying to present a lure to those spots. What casting angles would be best? How would you have to work the lure to get it close to the spots where the fish would be? Observe ... learn to visualize ... and then work at applying those same skills on the water.

Importance Of Record-Keeping

Catching bass is a rather simple proposition. Find the food and the best habitat option and you will most likely find fish. Execute the right presentation based on the details of the situation and the existing conditions, and you'll more than likely catch them.

By applying knowledge of the bass' seasonal behavior patterns to the available habitat and forage combinations, the task of narrowing the general location options becomes a fairly straightforward matter. Focusing on the existing conditions as they relate to the recent weather trends helps an angler choose appropriate presentations to the expected activity level of the fish in the positions judged to be worth investigating.

Haphazardly experimenting with a string of unrelated, narrowly applicable presentation/location possibilities is both time-consuming and frustrating. But conducting a logical sequence of experimental probes (casts/retrieves) can lead NAFC Members to the solutions.

By keeping track of the conditions, the steps taken in eliminating unproductive combinations of location, position and presentation, and the success or failure of those steps, anglers can build their own, personal knowledge base of bass behavior. It's that knowledge base that becomes the guide in expanding bass-fishing horizons.

Recording all this is an important step in the "higher education" of bass fishermen. To gain maximum benefit, more than a common fishing log is needed. The approach and passage of weather systems should be recorded daily, as well as the less obvious changes in the aquatic world that stem from or relate to those changes in weather, lunar forces or anything else. The discipline of maintaining these records forces one to take note of the natural

Pay attention to what is happening on shore. It's satisfying and it provides valuable clues on what's happening in the underwater world. By the way, can you spot the turkey?

Some Assembly Required

Once an angler puts it all together, catching bass becomes just another part of the overall activity, rather than an all-consuming goal. Catch-and-release fishing as a conservation measure becomes second nature.

cycles and the weather. The eventual goal is to become so familiar with these factors that they are felt as they happen and there is an awareness of their impending arrival, as well as an awareness of the likely effect on the aquatic ecosystem without having to refer to the notes or log.

The Final Step

The seemingly elusive goal of bass-fishing success comes easily with a thorough understanding of the aquatic ecosystem, and the role that bass play in it. All those tips and techniques that you've been exposed to begin to fit into the overall puzzle, as you begin to recognize the conditions that make them appropriate and when and where to apply them.

Something else comes with that understanding, as well. It's a sense of awe toward nature's incredible balancing act. At some point, it becomes natural for anglers to recognize the importance of minimizing their impact on the complex, interdependent relationships that make up the aquatic community. Each bass caught must be viewed as more than an accomplishment, and certainly more than someone's "property." Its value must be appreciated as an integral part of that environment. There is nothing inherently wrong with keeping a bass or two for the table, or with mounting a personal best. But the closer man comes to being in tune with the aquatic environment, the more man should feel like an actual part of it; thus, killing a bass unnecessarily becomes very much akin to destroying a part of himself.

As anglers grow toward the point where releasing their catch is as much a part of the sport as figuring out the answers, they should keep in mind that the worst crime against that aquatic ecosystem is the needless waste of a top-of-the-line predator. A bass you intend to eat is not necessarily wasted. A bass you kill just to prove you caught it, is.

A bigger loss yet is the bass that's killed through careless or reckless handling by the angler who cavalierly tosses it back while smugly congratulating himself for releasing it. There is a big difference between releasing a fish and throwing it back. That difference is a matter of purpose, ideals and technique. Too often it's a matter of life or death to the bass.

To maximize the practical effectiveness of your catch-and- release ideals, handle the fish as little as possible, and never squeeze its belly or grab its gills. Minimize the time it's out of the water and hold it upright in the water until it swims off on its own. Then get back to work using the information that that particular bass taught you to try to catch more! When you understand the aquatic environment, you can't help but marvel at it and respect it—and the individual fish that contribute to its balance.

Index